This book is dedicated to Arthur
Blessitt who God used to inspire and
influence my walk with Jesus,
and to my brilliant family.

Acknowledgements

Thankyou to my Mum and Dad, my wife Debbie and my family.
Also to my great Christian friends for their encouragement and love.
Special thanks to Jenny Nightingale, Mervyn and Lynn Smallwood, Mark
Lawson and Dave and Sandra Bailey for their practical help
and partnership in making this book a reality.

When God Takes Over

Lindsay Hamon

authorHOUSE®

AuthorHouse™
1663 Liberty Drive
Bloomington, IN 47403
www.authorhouse.com
Phone: 1-800-839-8640

Published by AuthorHouse 10/25/2012

ISBN: 978-1-4772-3883-7 (sc)
ISBN: 978-1-4772-3884-4 (e)

FORWARD

Lindsay Hamon has done those of us who believe in Jesus a great service in providing his extremely helpful book on evangelism. He writes neither as an armchair evangelist nor a distant observer but as a practitioner who is actually on the streets 'boots on the ground' doing the stuff!

As an equipping evangelist myself I have read over 75 books on the subject and this is one of the best, and here's why:

Lindsay is an excellent storyteller as well as an effective teacher as he gives theological insights without getting lost in the details, practical apologetic teaching without getting lost in the questions and real answers. He gives simple streetwise tips like how to get started in a witnessing conversation and 'how-to's' without sounding like a 'know-it-all', all the while realising that ultimately unless 'God takes over' all our efforts are in vain.

You may not be called to carry a 12-foot cross out on the streets like Lindsay, but as you slowly take in the truth in this book you will have Lindsay's passion for the salvation of souls burning in your heart.

Anglican minister Michael Green said "When men have a desire to make known the risen Lord they will find no shortage of ways to do it." We are free to find our own way or style of evangelism but we are not free to disobey Jesus' last command. 'When God Takes Over' will help you not only to obey, but to obey with joy!

Danny Lehmann
Evangelist, Youth With A Mission

PREFACE

I know of no greater happiness than that of telling others about Jesus! However, every time I go out to the streets or pubs to share the good news I feel so weak, so unprepared, so unable to do what Jesus has asked me to do. If only there was an expert around so that I could watch how it is supposed to be done. I would have loved to hide behind another person who possessed the confidence and 'know how' to skilfully lead people into a relationship with God. I could then hide behind them and watch them at work.

Over the years God has called me to be dependant on Him rather than on any human expert. Jesus told us to go and preach the good news to everyone yet He followed this by assuring us that He is with us always. As I walk behind Him onto the streets or into a bar I imagine Him whispering, 'Hide behind me, let me teach you, for I am gentle and humble of spirit.' This book is not written by a guy who knows what He's doing but by someone who is trying to learn that God knows what He's doing. I have tried to show that there is no exact formula or technique in sharing our faith but only the prompting and gentle instruction of Jesus our master craftsman. We are simply apprentices to Him and it is a joy to watch Him at work!

My hope is that the title of this book is reflected in the teachings and stories that are told. We go out in weakness and God takes over! I hope this book will inspire and encourage you to unashamedly share the good news of Jesus on the streets, in the pubs and clubs of our nation and beyond into the world. My prayer is that as you step out, God takes over!

"I am not ashamed of the good news about Christ.
It is the power of God at work, saving everyone who believes."
(Romans Chapter 1 v16a)

CONTENTS

CHAPTER 1

WHO DO YOU THINK YOU ARE?

The giant of Stockwell
The gangster of Soho
Upsetting everyone

The giant of Stockwell

Out of the corner of my eye I could see him looking at me.
Aware of how big he was, I could just make out the swallow
tattooed on his neck. I gulped hard on my coke and trying
not to look too nervous began praying hard. It seemed like
everyone had given me the once over when I entered the pub
and now this 'hulk Hogan' beside me was giving me 'the evils'. I
prayed harder and harder. I even tried praising God, seeking to
get up there in the 'heights of heaven', like a spitfire pilot getting
as high as he can before swooping down on an enemy fighter.
Sometimes we have to win the spiritual battle in our minds and
hearts before we open our mouths.

"Wot you doing 'ere? Never seen you in 'ere before."

A shot of adrenalin burst in my stomach. The tattooed man
was talking to me. "Where are you from?" he insisted.

"Mitcham," I mumbled, quickly sipping hard again on my
glass.

"Mitcham" he bellowed in his thick London accent. "That's
hundreds of miles away ... what you brings you 'ere?"

I decided to come clean. "God!" I squeaked in a barely
audible voice.

"God?" he shouted. By this time the whole pub could hear
our conversation. "Which God?" he demanded.

At that point something quite amazing happened. I

experienced what I could only describe as the 'mighty-mouse' phenomena. Feeling my chest puffing out, I suddenly stood upright (as high as my five foot seven inches would allow) and from nowhere I heard myself saying with a confidence and boldness that certainly was not from me, "The God, the God of Israel". I felt like David facing Goliath. Wow, that felt good! I really didn't expect it to come out like that. I never usually refer to God as the "God of Israel".

The man frowned, interrupting me before I could even get going. "I'm going to stop you there," he barked, and, lowering his voice, he confided that he was a very "naughty man". I was streetwise enough to know that 'naughty' in London parlance doesn't mean slightly mischievous in a lovable sort of a way. It meant that he was a criminal, a tough guy, a man not to be messed with. He confirmed this by saying, "People know me round 'ere, I've done time, the lot, know wot I mean?"

He then proceeded to tell me that he was going to share something with me and that I had better not laugh. I assured him with every bit of sincerity that I could muster that I would definitely not laugh at him, whatever he told me. He took a deep breath, and then embarked on his story. "Recently, I had a big row with my girlfriend, I was really cut up. I came in the pub and sat over there. I found myself kind of putting my hands in the air." He indicated a praying attitude with his hands open and slightly raised. "I looked up and said to God ... God, what's it all about? Just as I said that, I felt ... I felt ... well, I felt as God was all over me." He turned quickly to check that I wasn't laughing at him. "I felt Jesus, 'ere in this pub." He paused for a moment reliving the experience.

I was stunned!

"So then I got on the phone to the local vicar didn't I?!" he continued, "Vicar, I said, I'm not drunk, I'm not stoned, I've not taken anything but I think I've met Jesus."

"So now," he went on, "I've been going for lessons with the vicar about being a Christian. My life has changed and now my girlfriend has met God as well. Me bruvver came up to me the other day…ere he said, d'ya want do a job?" Again, I knew enough to know he didn't mean a legal job. "I told him I'd changed, that I was a new bloke. Now then my boy," he continued, towering above me, "Is that anything like wot you are talking about…?"

"Yes mate," I said, "it's exactly what I'm talking about."

Just then the guy spotted the pile of Christian leaflets I had on the bar. "What's these?" he asked grabbing a handful.

"Oh they are just leaflets explaining how you can meet God!" I gasped, still a bit overawed by his powerful story.

"Well, what're they doing on the bar? Let's give 'em out" he said, lumbering his frame round and thrusting a leaflet into the hands of everyone in the bar.

Fear had gripped me when I walked into the pub. I had

nothing but God, but He showed me that it's ok to feel weak and that He can use weakness to show that He is strong. I have never looked strong and have never felt strong. I haven't even got a strong before and after story. I am not a bad guy come good. I have always wished that I had an impressive story that would give me an authority on the streets, a kind of street-cred.

My story…? Well, I came to God at the age of six. No drugs, no drink, no naughties - asthmatic and skinny, a PE teacher's nightmare; the last to be picked at football. In fact, I possessed nothing at all that could score me macho points in the all-boys secondary school that I went to in the fast-growing London-over-spill town of Banbury, just on the edge of the Cotswolds.

The only thing I had going for me was that I could act, I could act the joker. I figured that if everyone's laughing at you, then they ain't beating you up! I'd go bright red even if a teacher spoke to me. Yet outside the classroom I'd act the part, 'ducking and diving' portraying a confidence that masked an overwhelming desire to be accepted.

At the age of eighteen years something profound happened. I felt the presence of Jesus for the first time in my life! Sitting on my motorbike on a Sunday night, Jesus gave me a taste of the peace of heaven. A Pentecostal pastor had prayed for me in the church an hour before and now here I was bathing in the Holy Spirit. "Can you feel God?" my girlfriend said from behind. The Lord was there! I'd always believed in Jesus but now I was feeling Him close to me. This is what I had been looking for.

That same year I'd seen Arthur Blessitt preach. Arthur is an American who has carried the cross around the world. There in Arthur's face was the radiance of Jesus. "I want what this man has got!" I prayed "I want to serve Jesus like that!" I didn't realise that God would hold me to that prayer and I would seek to live a life constantly sharing the same Jesus that Arthur has faithfully served.

We don't have to be strong but we do need to know this strong Jesus who has all authority in heaven and earth. We may not have a heavy duty conversion story but we serve a 'heavy duty' God. Maybe you are like me, weak physically, weak emotionally, you may even feel weak spiritually, then you must realise just who it is who lives in your heart, who it is that you work for.

The gangsters of Soho

A good friend of mine, John Pressdee, tells a story of when he was driving down a narrow street in Soho. To his dismay, the door of a parked car opened in front of him, he collided into it smashing the door mirror. Being a pastor, he thought he better stop but soon wished he had carried on down the road. Out of the car came four men in black, dark glasses, suits, the lot, they looked like they had just walked off the set of a gangster movie. The only problem was they hadn't. This was for real. They crowded around John. He knew he was in trouble. Suddenly he found himself saying to the men, "Do you realise who I am?"

The men looked at each other, this ploy had at least stalled them.

He took a slightly different tack. "Do you realise who I work for?" This was club land and it mattered who you worked for.

The guys were getting a little jittery.

John decided to let them have it. "I work for the highest authority in the land." He paused for breath, "I work for Jesus Christ!". As he said that, the men in black took a visible step back, just as happened when the guards had come to arrest Jesus and Jesus had said "I am He," (John Chapter 18 V 5-6).

"We are so sorry," the suits said to John. "Please come and meet our boss." Their boss was a club land manager. In a subsequent meeting with the manager it became apparent that in the club land circle managers can't afford to have too many real friends and even with their friends, they would be reluctant to show any weakness. For a time John operated as an unofficial chaplain for the club land fraternity who respected the authority of Jesus that they saw in him. Each one of us must recognise just who lives in us; "the highest authority in the land," the Lord of heaven's armies, the God of Israel.

Upsetting everyone

"I could never talk to a total stranger about my faith! I wouldn't know what to say…"

"How do you start such a conversation anyway? I couldn't face the embarrassment if they told me they were not interested…"

"People can get very funny about religion! Doesn't it get to you when people reject you…?"

"…anyway, surely people would go to church if they were interested in God. They don't want you stopping them when they are shopping."

"I avoid anyone who does surveys…"

"…and it's not good talking to anyone in a pub or a club, they don't want you ruining their evening by being forced into having some deep and meaningful conversation, they just want to relax."

"People are often drunk and abusive in pubs and will just make fun of you. Besides, often the music is too loud! I know one bloke who got thumped in one pub for talking religion…"

I've heard all these statements. I've even said them to myself: "Don't talk to anyone on the streets or in the pub… Definitely don't go door-to-door, that's what Jehovah's Witnesses do, and we all know what everyone thinks of them…! Don't talk to people in parks; people will think you are a pervert… You can't talk to people on trains, buses or at an airport or people will be scared of you... You have to realise you can't invade people's airspace!"

If you listen to every negative statement, the truth is, you would rarely witness to anyone and especially not to the general public. Many Christians have told me that the best way to see people commit themselves to Jesus is through personal friendships. Statistically this appears to be true. More people are apparently won in that way than in any other way. However, does that mean that sharing your faith in public doesn't work...?

Getting thrown out

I have a sensitive, artistic temperament and can be acutely aware of the embarrassment that people feel when I talk about Jesus. On more than one occasion I have been punched, thrown over and escorted out of bars by security simply for sharing Jesus.

Our local nightclub had an enormous Afro-Caribbean man who spoke with a Cornish accent. His weekends would be spent on door security manhandling drunk, aggressive Cornish lads out of the club when their behaviour had become totally unsocial. Most of the club goers were happy to let me talk to them about Jesus, although some of them were so drunk or deaf - the loud music didn't help - that they thought I was talking about "cheeses" not "Jesus". Every so often one of the club goers would complain to management and, despite my gentle approach, I would be accused of 'shoving religion down people's throats'. Before long the security staff learnt how to locate me in the bustling club. They would just follow the path of colourful Christian leaflets strewn across tables and they would track me down. This would put the big Cornish Caribbean 'bouncer' in a predicament. His mother was a full-on spirit-filled Pentecostal lady, and she would not be happy at all about her son throwing out the preacher. In the Caribbean, preachers are given respect and the poor man would plead with me to leave peacefully and not give them trouble.

"My mother would never forgive me for throwing out the preacher," he would mumble under his breath, in his Cornish Caribbean accent.

On more than one occasion club goers have followed me out of the pub or club to see why I was being thrown out and I have continued to preach outside.

Brixton bus

Once I jumped on a bus at Brixton tube station. I was on my way to visit a prisoner at Brixton jail, only a short bus ride away. As I got on the bus I couldn't help sensing that the atmosphere on the bus was awful. I'm not as sensitive as some at discerning spiritual atmospheres but this was so strong even I knew something was wrong. I was full of the joy of the Lord at that time, so I leapt to the front of the bus and announced to the passengers, "There is a terrible atmosphere on this bus!"

This was not my usual way of starting a preach, but it caught people's attention. I launched into a gospel preach and began to get very excited about telling the passengers about the joy that Jesus could bring into our lives. Once the bus conductor recovered from the shock of hearing someone preaching on his bus, he hastened to shut me up immediately.

Well he wasn't counting on the presence of a large Caribbean lady. She insisted in no uncertain terms that the preacher should be allowed to preach. As soon as she had said her piece, a very respectable lady announced that she was an atheist and didn't believe any of this "nonsense". A Catholic lady then joined in, saying that while she did believe in God, religion should be kept in churches where it belongs. Well, that was like a red-rag to a bull. The Caribbean lady was really getting all fired up now. This was the Jeremy Kyle and the Jerry Springer shows all rolled in one. It seemed that everyone was having their say. Just as I thought that tempers would be lost, I suddenly realised that we had arrived at Brixton Prison.

"Bye everyone!" I shouted, leaving the heated debate in full flow. They were still arguing over whether or not the preacher should be allowed to preach Jesus in public. I will never know whether it ended in blows but it had certainly put the cat amongst the pigeons.

Tapping the arteries

Back in the late-eighties I felt a strange calling to preach Jesus on the Underground network in London. The phrase that had entered my mind was that God had wanted to tap the arteries of the heart of this land for Jesus. I fought the calling, not wishing to leave beautiful Cornwall and its stunning rocky coastline. The idea of taking the family with three primary school age kids at that time to the big smoke was daunting. A few months later a house became available, rent-free and we made the big decision to rent out our house in Cornwall and start a new life in South London in an area called Mitcham, near Croydon. I would spend all my days riding the Underground with a go-anywhere ticket, preaching on the platforms in the two-to-three minutes of waiting time between trains. It's amazing how much of the gospel you can pack in to a couple of minutes.

British reserve was on my side and people would usually stay totally quiet while I delivered my message. I must have preached to representatives of almost every nation over the four and half years I was there. Pure adrenalin would pulse through me most of the time. Each time I preached I had to battle internal 'collywobbles' beforehand. Once I'd opened with, "…Ladies and gentleman…" I would be committed and off I would go preaching.

I suffered from countless throat and chest infections and after several visits to my Jewish doctor , he suggested with a knowing twinkle in his eye that my 'boss' should perhaps give me a new job, based on health and safety grounds. Despite the demands of the work thousands heard and, I hope, took on board the short gospel preaches. God was tapping the arteries of the heart of the UK. Often I would just ride the trains and talk to whoever was sitting next to me. Contrary to what you may understandably think, many people actually wanted to talk with me. Many times I had the joy of leading people in prayer to accept Jesus. I remember on one occasion a person began to follow me in a simple prayer of commitment when the tube train stopped in a tunnel and everybody was totally quiet. All that could be heard was the two of us praying through that beautiful prayer to receive Jesus.

Often I would be accompanied by others who had a story to share. These included, among others, my good friend, Pete, an ex-boxer who would tenaciously share Jesus from morning to night; Shirley, a nurse who gave up all her spare time between nursing shifts to share her Jesus. There was an opera singer whose singing would shake countless Tube windows when she gave her rendition of Amazing Grace. She would follow this by sharing her story of how, after being mugged on the Tubes, she started seeking Jesus. There was also the wife of a man dying of multiple sclerosis who testified publicly how God gave her the strength to carry on. There were youth workers, pastors, musicians, students, even a guy from Germany who spent a week sharing his story on the tube platforms. Exciting times! It was almost too exciting, leaving me exhausted at night, I would often fall asleep while reading my kids a bedtime story, "Dad ... what happens next...?"

Nightmare comes true

I used to have a reoccurring dream that a demonized man would attack me, seeking to strangle me in the dream. I would not be able to get out the words, "I bind you in Jesus' name", out. I would awake in a cold sweat just before he succeeded in strangling me.

London can be an aggressive place at times and I recall one violent young man who seemed intent on shutting me up. It seemed that he appeared to be held on his seat when I had bound the spirit controlling him. I cannot say I am adept at handling these situations; I just seem to fly by the 'seat of my pants' most of the time. I am rarely totally sure if I am doing the right thing and as I often work alone it isn't always possible to consult a human 'expert'. Often the only advisor around is the Holy Spirit.

Eventually the day came when my reoccurring dream became a reality. I had just begun what, I hope, was a very gentle, loving preach to one half of the train carriage. I talked of Jesus' love for us, the penalty of our own sin, God's desire to forgive and cleanse us should we turn to him. The message was not provocative in any way, or at least not in the human sense. With no warning, a guy in his thirties sprung to his feet and launched himself at me. I remember being shocked to see that his pupils were so dilated that I couldn't see the whites of his eyes at all. This was my dream becoming reality. Instantly the words came out of my mouth, "I bind you in Jesus' name!" To my utter dismay ... nothing happened! He kept coming! I felt cheated! It didn't work! Where was the spiritual warfare manual telling me what to do in the event of failure? The man grabbed my throat and we began to waltz around the carriage. He didn't seem to have any power in his hands but even so, I was still concerned about how this would all end up.

My good friend, Pete, was busy sharing Jesus with everyone in the next carriage when a little voice sprung into his head, "... Don't talk to that person! Lindsay needs your help next door." He waited until the train stopped at a station and changed carriages, only to see me anxiously going through my Strictly-Come-Dancing routine with the demon-crazed man. Pete had done boxing and knew how to handle himself but in the event, his prowess was not needed. Instead, a member of the public sprang to my rescue and managed to place himself between the two of us. It would be great if I could say that the whole incident had a triumphant ending and that the demonized man was delivered on the spot. He wasn't. All I recall was that my 'rescuer' turned to me and said "Don't think I'm into religion or anything but I just don't like scum like that picking on little guys like you." He might not have been a Christian or pro-Jesus, but God used him anyway and I was very grateful!

Do it anyway

Despite all opposition from the public the Bible makes it clear that the purpose of our salvation is not something that we should just keep to ourselves. God wants us to share our relationship with Him with the world. I often tell people that the most selfish thing we could ever do would be to keep the cure for cancer to ourselves. The Gospel is a heaven or hell thing. Are we going to keep the goodness of heaven to ourselves? When our child scoffs a whole box of chocolates to himself without sharing with his friends we have a go at him for being totally selfish. Are we selfish about the Gospel? God wants us to share it! Often the reason why we have found God is because someone has told us about Him. The truth is that the Holy Spirit reveals Jesus to us and He wants us to continue to speak about Jesus to others. Indeed, He leaps for joy within us when we do. I for one am only really content when I am sharing Jesus.

CHAPTER 2

BREAKING DOWN BARRIERS

What do you say to start off
The power of your own story
Something happens when you pray

What do you say to start off?

This is the first question that I am most often asked by Christians who want to reach out on the streets. The true answer to that question is that I can't actually remember what I say to start off because I never know what I am going to say before I say it! When carrying the cross I shake everyone's hand and then hold onto it long enough to at least say, "God Bless You." I often follow this with, "I bet I'm the first person today to tell you that God loves you!" I guess people would almost expect you to say something like that when you are carrying a 12 foot cross!

The important question isn't so much the exact words you say but how you say them. The whole deal is what's in your heart. Do you really believe that God loves them? Do you really have a heart of love for people?

Love 'em all

Year after year I would take the cross to the Glastonbury Festival. I became known as 'The Cross Man', and I'm told that there is a short clip of the cross being carried on the official Glastonbury film. Glastonbury Festival is great when it's sunny but probably more resembles the First World War trenches when it rains and trudging through ankle-deep mud all weekend isn't a picnic. To get told endlessly by drunk or stoned characters that Jesus "never had a wheel on His cross" becomes a little tedious at times.

On occasions I confess to being guilty of thinking, "these guys are just a bunch of drunken wasters." One year I met a man who helped change me totally. He set me free and I will always be grateful to him. He stood there, grinning from ear to ear, dressed up as a clown collecting money for Romanian orphans. What a guy! He loved Jesus with all his heart and was so pleased to see the cross being carried. "Aren't these kids great?" he said enthusiastically. "I don't know why they love an old 'fart' like me… I love them to bits," he went on, and then added, "They are so generous to me."

I made out that I agreed with him but inside I realised that I was so uptight and judgemental towards the teenagers that he loved. I didn't have to be very bright to realise why the Glastonbury kids loved him so much - he loved them! It changed my life. I now ask God for His love for everyone - and I mean everyone; the teenagers, the grandparents, the drunks, the beggars, the shopkeepers, the mums, the jokers and the serious. He wants us to "love 'em all, the big, the fat and the small". I'm sure you can get the spirit of this! God's love sets us free to be ourselves and even to have a sense of humour.

I have found that shaking everyone's hand is powerful. Those who are antagonistic will refuse to shake my hand. It hurts a bit, sure, but there's always the next guy and he might be the one who asks you why you are carrying a massive cross on your shoulders.

At the end of the day the only way to engage with someone is to greet them in some way. Most of us aren't too scared to ask someone directions to find a certain road. "Excuse me," we'll say, stopping a total stranger in their tracks. For me saying "Excuse me", kick starts me into having to say something. Once I've said "Excuse me", I'm committed to talking to them. Of course, I could 'wimp out' and meekly ask them if they have the time.

In the pub I'll often go over to a person at the bar and simply say, "I've just come over to say hello." I'm always totally upfront with people. I tell them exactly what I'm about, "I'm talking to people about being born-again."

If I'm with a friend, I might say, "Hi can I introduce my friend to you, do you mind if he tells you his story of how he met God?" Although this approach is confrontational or in-your-face, I've found it helpful to be transparently honest about why I want to talk to them. It's understandable that a stranger would want to know your reason for talking to them.

In your face or softly softly?

Some Christians are very embarrassed about my forward approach, saying that it is too direct. They say it has a high squirm factor. Some prefer a far more subtle approach. They talk about the weather, politics, football, cricket, any bit of small talk and then pray that the conversation will naturally come around to religion. My good friend, John Pressdee, is very good at this. He is a pastor and great at talking with anybody. In fact he is the type of guy that could talk about anything with anybody at any time. I remember being with him in a pub in Europe where most people seemed to speak English. John had started some deep discussion with one of the customers about jazz. I knew nothing about jazz and made some excuse to leave and wandered around the pub and tried (unsuccessfully) to engage the other customers with talk of Jesus. I came back an hour later quite deflated, only to find John with his hand on the customer's shoulder praying his heart out for him. John had built up trust with the individual before venturing into the more personal areas of faith. "Softly, softly to catch a monkey," is the phrase that is used.

I've tried being more laid-back. I have tried, I really have, but I have found that I am just no good at it. In my experience using the softly-softly approach often results in softly, softly catching nothing and seems to waste an awful lot of time in the process. We all have to be comfortable to do things in a way suitable to our personality. However, especially on the streets I maintain that it is important to be direct to put people at ease. People may think you are trying to chat them up or sell them something. Most of us have our barriers up when a total stranger approaches us; it's the law of the jungle. In big cities people are especially on their guard and suspicious.

I use humour a lot. In fact I'm not too good at relating to people who haven't got a sense of humour. I'm not sure if Jesus did too well with the uptight and miserable, look at His interactions with the stuffy Pharisees! When people want to know what I'm about I've been known to tell them that I'm the local 'Bible basher', or I'm the 'religious nutter'. It makes them laugh and barriers come tumbling down.

I remember giving out Christian leaflets to a long queue of prison visitors at Wandsworth Prison. I was left with one leaflet which I was still clutching as I entered the prison. At the door there was a gruff, Cockney prison guard. On seeing the leaflet in my hands, he turned to his mates and said, "This bloke's got a leaflet as well ... who's the religious pervert giving out all these things?" I bottled out from admitting that it was me, (shame on you Linds!).

Being relaxed and enjoying yourself can cause some people problems. They can't put you in a box. I am dressed in jeans and a hoodie and am joking.

"You probably think I am trying to convert you ... well ... I am," I'll say. People will laugh and won't initially believe that I am a Christian. It is not until I produce a Bible do they realise I am not 'winding them up'. I am actually a full-on Bible believing born-again Christian. The apostle Paul became like people on the outside in order to reach them on the inside.

Once I've introduced myself, I find that a good way of getting straight to the point, is to ask a question. "Do you know what it means to be born again?" is a favourite. I've even asked that question while waiting next to a total stranger to cross the road. We've ended up walking together quite a way chatting through about the Gospel. I might say to someone, "Can I have a chat to you about Jesus?" followed by a further question, "Do you have any faith yourself?"

Open or closed?

Generally speaking, I find people quite quickly show which side of the fence they are going to drop down on; some do it in a direct way, swearing at you, others do it politely. I've found it's possible to pick up very quickly if they really have no time for God. I've found that some Christians do not pick up the 'not interested' signs and keep trying for too long. When someone is open to God it can be an absolute pleasure talking to them.

I've noticed an interesting phenomena. If a person isn't open to God, I don't seem to be able to flow in the Spirit. The Holy Spirit isn't into wasting time and if the person isn't interested, the Spirit won't flow. The Bible teaches that, if anything, the Spirit is actually blinding them from the truth because their hearts are hard. "Harden the hearts of these people, plug their ears and shut their eyes, that way they will not see with their eyes or hear with their ears, nor understand with their hearts and turn to me for healing." (Isaiah Chapter 6 verse 10).

On the other hand, when people are open to God, I find that suddenly, I get the 'gift of the gab'. I find myself flowing in the Spirit and, on occasions, can't believe the stuff that comes out of my mouth. "Where did that come from?" I muse to myself, "That bit of wisdom was too wise to come from my mind." Sometimes God talks directly to the open-minded person and that is why you can't remember what you said afterwards. The Holy Spirit has spoken through you, but not via your brain!

What often happens is that the Holy Spirit speaks into their mind, revealing the truth to them. How many of us congratulate the preacher for saying something he doesn't recall even saying? Sometimes we don't even voice the words but the Holy Spirit still speaks directly. It happens, and it is God doing His own thing.

The other day I spoke to a 13 year old boy and explained the Gospel to him. All his friends had run off at the earliest opportunity, leaving the poor lad alone. The boy was not fazed by this at all and clearly began to finish off every sentence as I went through the Gospel message. There was an 'inside communicator' revealing the truth to the lad. Jesus said, "For no one can come to me unless the Father who sent Me draws them to Me, and at the last day I will raise them up" (John Chapter 6 v 44).

Often we reprimand ourselves if the conversation isn't fruitful, saying, "I used the wrong approach, if only I'd said things better, I made a right hash of that one!" Similarly, when the conversation goes well we congratulate ourselves feeling "I did well there!" The truth is, it was the Holy Spirit who did well.

If the receiver is working, God will send His radio waves. If it is closed He won't. "Apart from Me, you can do nothing." says Jesus. (John Chapter 15 v 5b)

One of the most famous questions is, of course, "If you die tonight would you know for certain that you would go to heaven?" The response to this type of question reveals where the person is spiritually. Some feel that they are going to heaven based on them being good, or being very 'religious'. Some hope that they are going to heaven, but have no assurance. Some joke they are probably going to hell because they are so bad. Some just don't know. Whatever their response, it opens up the possibility of you explaining the Gospel.

"Would you like me to explain to you how you can know for certain that you are going to heaven?" I often go on to ask.

The book Evangelism Explosion* by Kennedy outlines in great detail how we can explain the Gospel, based on this approach. However, we must be careful that we don't work by technique alone, but by the Holy Spirit.

Jehovah Witnesses are often adept at manoeuvring their listener down a particular path to coral them into a corner. Clever arguing of this type isn't the way of the Spirit. If God is drawing someone to himself we don't have to rely on skilled manipulation to assist Him. I am not, of course, saying that argument and

* Evangelism Explosion, James Kennedy, Tyndale

debate don't have their place; God used Paul's gifts in this way very effectively. It's just that I have found that it is God's spirit, not just the logic of human argument that brings a person to God.

German experiment

Many years ago I was asked to take a seminar on street evangelism in Germany. I never feel confident in such circles, feeling that other Christians are more learned than myself. Maybe this is a product of attending a very working class school rather than a posh grammar school. Shortly before leaving school the system became comprehensive and these class barriers were largely broken. I am not a theologian or even an ordained minister and to be faced with a room full of very serious and intense pastors filled me with a sense of inadequacy "Why did I say yes to this?" I muttered to myself under my breath.

"Street Evangelism!" I announced. The pastors looked over their half-rimmed glasses expecting an academic lecture on the subject. "You can't teach street evangelism in a classroom any more than you can teach someone to drive in a classroom."

The pastors seemed intrigued by my introduction but soon their expressions reflected a picture of total panic as they heard what I was proposing. There were about thirty of them present and I told them to get into groups of three.

Their task was to go out into the streets with a view to stopping a member of the public, introducing themselves and then asking them two questions. The first pastor was to ask the person if he minded one of his colleagues taking a couple of minutes to explain how he came to commit his life to Jesus. Once this was done, the next pastor was to ask them if he or she minded them saying a prayer for them.

Well, I could see, even without understanding the German language, that they were not at all happy with my proposal. However, German formality and politeness left them with no alternative than to obey my suggestion. Off they went like frozen- faced penguins into the night.

I told them to be back by a certain time. Now Germans are famous for their time-keeping but that night they were nowhere to be seen at the time of the allotted homecoming. What could have happened to them? Had they voted with their feet and skived off my training session?

Gradually they drifted back but no longer the sour faced intellectuals. They were laughing and talking excitedly to each other, recounting the night's events. What a transformation! Little by little the stories would come in, like soldiers coming back from an exciting raid. It turned out that each of the ten groups that went out had, during the hour of their exercise, testified to and prayed with at least three sets of people, many of them stopping couples. This meant that, in one hour, some thirty to sixty people heard a testimony and had been prayed with by a group of pastors. More importantly, the pastors had a taste of being 'pastors of the street' not just purveyors of academic theology. They had come alive and only laughter and joy emanated from them on their return.

Leaflets

In the past, my perception of street-evangelism was centred mainly around the idea of feverishly handing out as many Christian leaflets as possible, in order to reach as many people as possible in the time allotted. The hope was that they would read the leaflet, pray the prayer at the end of the message and then contact the telephone number to say they wanted to hear more. This rarely happened in my experience; however this doesn't mean that leaflets do not have their place in the process of sharing the good news. Both businesses and political parties know the effectiveness of using leaflets to advertise their message or products.

Leaflets can be left anywhere, buses, trains, laundrettes, libraries, etc. If a leaflet is well produced it can be a useful evangelism tool. Personally, I find using leaflets gives me an excuse to talk to someone. I use them as a security blanket to help me to get going. I've found that I witness to far more people with my back pocket full of leaflets than I do without them.

I had my conversion story printed. I ordered thousands of copies; in fact so many that I am still giving the same ones out now twenty years later! It is easy to take a photograph of yourself and write a three-paragraph conversion story on the back, get it printed and off you go. At the supermarket, slip the girl your story on the printed postcard. Do the same at the petrol station, and at the post office and then give one to the bus driver on the way home. In fact, everywhere you go keep giving them out saying, "Have a copy of my story, it's how I came to know Jesus". It will free you up big time.

Sure, you'll still battle with the fear factor as soon as you decide to give out a leaflet. What you have to realise that the devil is fighting hard for you to keep those leaflets in your back pocket.

It is important to remember that none of us know what is going on in the life of that supermarket girl or the guy at the petrol station. He might have Christian grandparents praying for him every day and by giving that leaflet to that young girl or guy, you might be an answer to their prayer.

Where possible, I always try to mention the name of Jesus when I give out testimony leaflets, after all our conversion story is not our story but Jesus' story. It's how Jesus changed us. It is not to do with pushing ourselves or bigging ourselves up.

If you merely just give out leaflets the dynamics can sometimes militate against you from engaging with the person. They simply lower their eyes to the leaflet and off they go focussing on the leaflet. If the leaflet is simply stuffed in their pocket then it often ends up as a solid lump of paper when it comes out of the washing machine at the end of the week.

To avoid this happening, I usually say, "Can I give you this leaflet and I wonder if you could read it and tell me what you think?" Most people are happy to do that for you. While they think they are doing you a favour, the dynamics change and they feel less threatened. You are not imposing your beliefs on them, you are asking for their reaction to your experience of Jesus. While they are reading your leaflet you can be praying hard for them under your breath that the Holy Spirit would work on them as they read it.

Once they have read through the leaflet I ask them if they have had any dealings with God themselves or if they would like to receive Jesus into their lives.

Some have expressed a very cynical viewpoint about the use of leaflets.

"For God so loved the world…" quoting from John Chapter 3 v 16, "that He gave *a leaflet*".

They've made their point, God sent His Son, not a leaflet. They usually then go on to say that they are more into 'presence evangelism' or if they are even more articulate and more academic use the phrase 'incarnational evangelism'. If you don't know what that means ask a theologian and he will tell you that it is something about God living amongst us. We do have the responsibility of being a representative of God, and of having

His Spirit living in us and moving through us. This, of course, is absolutely true, we can be the mouthpiece, the arms, hands and feet of God. His love should shine through us. I have seen Jesus shining through people's eyes and through their lives. People can't see God but they can see you, and you might be the only 'vision' of God that they see.

Words or actions?

"Preach the Gospel and, if necessary, use words!" I believe St Francis is quoted as saying something to that effect. However if we use this line of thinking to refrain from using words, we end up talking to fewer and fewer people about Jesus. We are always hoping that people will think our lives are so different that they will end up asking why we are as we are. We hang onto the theory that this will finally give us a chance to say our bit for Jesus. I know that this can happen but I can only say that this has rarely happened to me. (Maybe the reason for this is that my life is not always so radically different from my non-believing friends, some of whom act far more unselfishly and are more loving than myself.)

At the end of the day Jesus used words like "preach" and "witness" and "testify". This means what it says! *Use words.* The devil hates the "Word of God" whether or not it comes through the written word or the living word being heard from the mouths of believers. The constant battle in our mind is "Don't talk! Don't mention Jesus! Don't say you're a Christian, etc" We swallow this stuff and find ourselves apologising for preaching, "Don't think I'm preaching or anything" we say as if preaching is a dirty word. No, good preaching is inspired and empowered by God Himself. Use godliness, holiness, compassion to live out what you believe but also use words...... words are powerful!

Questionnaires

One method I have used to help kick-start me is to use a questionnaire. The pub questionnaire starts with very non-threatening questions about a person's life and then goes on to ask a series of questions including: "Do you ever feel ashamed of your past life?" or "Who is Jesus according to your belief?" One of the best questions is, "If you could know God personally would you be interested?" To my surprise, most people answer "yes" to that one. It gives a great opening to ask if they mind me sharing how I came to know God. The dynamics are right; they are asking me to tell them about my experience. I can then go on to tell them my story of conversion.

I am always aware that it is possible to hide behind the questionnaire. The questionnaire is not an end in itself; it is merely a 'security blanket' again to help you get going sharing Jesus. When people ask me what the questionnaire is about I say that, "It's about you and your life". Sometimes I will then go on to say that it's an excuse to say what Jesus has done for me. "What has Jesus done for you?" people may reply. Off I'll go, sharing my story. The questionnaire will then be totally forgotten.

The reason for the questionnaire is not to collect statistics on belief, but rather as a means to sharing the gospel. I have mixed with some very high powered Christians who can at times present as quite a high flying breed. Some of them have denigrated the use of leaflets and questionnaires as being very worldly tools, preferring the use of words of knowledge, prophesy and healing as the more 'heavy duty tools of the Spirit'. I agree with them but I am not always that 'powerful'. Sometimes a leaflet or a questionnaire can kick start me to witness especially in the UK, where, by and large, people are very reserved and often embarrassed to talk about God. I very rarely get words of knowledge and have been totally amazed when it has happened. I know that if I did get a word about someone I'd probably be scared to give it. What happens if I'm wrong? I have actually given words to members of the public that have been wrong and, to my surprise they have been very gracious about my mistake. However, there have been a few occasions when the word was accurate.

Words that are active

I was in a pub in Islington with Christians from the local Anglican church. I had worked all the way around the pub giving out leaflets and talking to most of the customers, except one. She was the lady sitting by the piano all evening. To be honest I bottled out of giving her a leaflet. You know when people give off those vibes, "Just don't talk to me, just don't you dare come near me." Well she was one of those. When I approach these types I almost always get my head bitten off. In this instance I gave this hard-faced, bitter lady a wide berth.

On leaving the pub I called in the local pizza parlour to meet my friend Ali, an Iranian refugee, who had been given political asylum in the UK after being tortured in his own country. He had accepted Jesus after I prayed for him to be able to cry. The Holy Spirit had filled the pizza parlour and Ali had started to sob uncontrollably letting out years of pain. It was so moving. After that experience Ali was quick to accept Jesus and we became friends. He used to have a pizza waiting for me every time I visited.

On this particular night I was queuing up in his pizza parlour to meet him, when who should walk in but our sour-faced lady from the pub...... the 'ice queen' herself. To my horror, she recognised me.

"I know who you are……….. you're that little religious pervert from the pub."

Not content at reducing me to two inches tall before the crowd, she started to rant at the top of her voice, "Where was God when I was bringing up my kids on my own, answer me that?"

On and on she went, venting her fury against God and her disdain for people like me 'who were so weak that they needed to dream up some idea of there being a God.'

During her tirade the word 'cancer' came into my mind. "I can't tell her that she has cancer, what if I'm wrong?" I thought. After churning this around in my mind, I figured I would dress things up a bit to lessen the shock if I was wrong. "I can see how you think that you've coped without God so far but what happens if something terrible happens to you, like getting cancer?"

There, 'cancer'. I'd said the word. Well the reaction was unbelievable. The woman crumpled almost in front of my eyes. Her emotional armour-plating fell to the floor at her feet. Her eyes filled with tears. Suddenly I was looking at a little child and my heart filled with love for her.

"Well," she gasped, "maybe that's true, but ..."

The words trailed off, and muttering something about, '… having a problem like that…' she left the shop.

I wish now that I had chased after her but my head was still reeling from what just had happened. The Word of God is alive and active! "For whatever God says is full of living power, it is sharper than the sharpest dagger, cutting swift and deep into our innermost thoughts and desires with all their parts exposing us for what we really are." (Hebrews Chapter 4 v12)

Words of knowledge are so powerful and I'm always praying for that gift.

On one occasion, my wife, Debbie, interrupted me in full flow while I was seeking to lead a student in the sinner's prayer. A holy moment!

I was taken aback that Debbie would seek to interrupt such a moment. "You can't pray with Lindsay can you because you have a voice in your head telling you that we are lying to you and you don't trust us?" She then offered to pray with him to ask God to remove that voice.

As we prayed the second time, immediately there was the heaviest feeling of the presence of the Holy Spirit.

I had been sharing Jesus off and on for almost twenty years at that college and this was the most amazing incident ever. God's Holy Presence in that student common room area. He was there in power. The student left and we heard, weeks later, that he had gone into his classroom and told his mates that some "Bible bashers" had prayed over him and he had really experienced God in a big way, he'd changed and that he was really happy. One of his fellow students went on to find God as a result of hearing this. The word of knowledge is so effective!

During the same few weeks my wife had received a vision of a student that she believed we would meet and that she would be found near the Art block. I am not very good at people telling me what to do especially when I'm out specifically sharing Jesus.

I like to 'duck and dive' according to the sensitivity of the Spirit but on this occasion I obeyed Debbie. Sure enough, the very girl appeared, coming out of the Art block, exactly as Debbie had seen her in her vision. Dressed in black Gothic garb, she spat out confidently, "You can't come near me, I'm a satanist."

"That doesn't matter darling," my wife began. "Jesus went into hell for you!"

I was surprised at Debbie's boldness, she normally speaks quite timidly. This time Debbie was on a roll and you couldn't shut her up. She went on and on preaching to the girl. Students were now pouring out of the college block and a small crowd began to gather bemused by Debbie's speech.

Some students began to mock her, oozing cynicism. They then tried to interrupt. To our amazement the Satanist turned on her heels and told her friends to shut up and listen to what Debbie had to say.

Eventually Debbie began to pray for the group. The girls began to giggle but our Satanist friend reprimanded them telling them to keep quiet. When it was all over the Satanist hugged us warmly, gone was her hardness, a new softness was on her. She wasn't yet ready to give her life to Jesus but God had done something remarkable.

Remember it is God that wants to break down the barriers even more than us. He will often do everything He can to hand the situation to us on a plate.

Handed on a plate

I had just finished giving a small group of teenagers some simple training on sharing their faith. The idea was that they would then go out on the streets to find young people of their age to talk to.

We had just walked out of the church when two young people walked through the church car park. I called them over and asked if we could use them as part of our training. I explained to them that the group of teenagers were wanting to share their faith but were a bit nervous about getting started, would they mind if we used them as guinea pigs for the young people to practise on? They knew me from taking school assemblies and one of them had attended the open youth club at the church.

"It's funny you should call me over because recently I've been thinking about God", said one of the guys.

One of the Christian girls shared her personal story of finding faith, just as she had done only moments before in the training session. I asked the boys if they would like to receive Jesus and, to our amazement, they said "yes". They were completely sincere and after a short time were ready to pray with us. God had handed the incident to us on a plate!

On another occasion, I had been praying on my own in the church, imploring God to "save souls". On leaving the church, I saw a tough looking guy taking a short cut through the church car park.

"Stop the car and talk to him!" the Spirit urged me.

God is our Commanding Officer and when He says "jump" we should say "how high?" We shouldn't wait even a minute. We must often frustrate God when we dilly dally around and we miss the opportunities He lays on for us.

On this occasion I didn't blow it but shot out of the car and explained to the man that God had told me to talk to him. To be honest, I wasn't exactly sure what God wanted to say to him. He looked at me blankly.

I noticed that he had three tear drops tattooed just down from his left eye and I asked him what these tattoos signified. He began to tell me that his wife had died, his mother had died and he had also lost a child.

I prayed for him.

Tears, real ones, not tattoos, fell from his eyes. I thought he would give his life to Jesus but he wouldn't despite me imploring him to do so.

"I'll do it when I get home!" he said. I know when the apple is ready it comes off the tree easily. He wasn't ready yet. Nevertheless, God had reached into his pain and sorrow.

I remember walking past a pub with the cross in Gwalchmai, on the Isle of Anglesey in North Wales. I had been carrying the cross all week, making my way from mid-Wales to Queensferry where there was going to be a Luis Palau evangelistic event; 'Tell

Wales'. I was due to talk with young people at a church in the evening but had most of the Sunday free to carry the cross to Holyhead.

As I passed a pub, a minibus stopped and out came a local Rugby team, big guys, very rough and very Welsh. I wimped out of talking with them and made to walk past, figuring they would just make fun of me.

"Oi!" I heard from behind "What you doing with that cross?"

"I'm carrying it!"

"We can see that you xxx idiot!" "Where are you carrying it to?

"Holyhead!" I said meekly.

"Where have you come from?"

"Llandrindod Wells!"

"Llandrindod Wells?......... That's hundreds of miles away, you could do with a drink, come on, bring the cross in the pub!"

It wasn't every Sunday the local rugby team arrived at the pub with a twelve foot cross under their arms...... doors flung open and the team wasted no time in manoeuvring the cross to a central position around the corner from the bar.

To my utter dismay the pub was jammed packed full that morning. Everybody was there, old people, teenagers and whole families. When the cross was brought in the whole pub erupted!

From nowhere, one of the rugby players produced a chain

saw, started it up and made out that he was going to chop up the cross. I was aghast, but I couldn't show my concern.

"A little bit off every corner would do nicely thank you", I said, concealing my true feelings.

"Fair play!" they said, putting the saw down and slapping me on the back.

"Now boy, what you having to drink?"

"Make it a coke, I don't want to be done by the police, drunk in charge of a cross!" They liked that and I began to relax.

I had a whole bunch of 'Journey Into Life*' booklets, a sort of cartoon explanation of the Gospel, written by a guy called Norman Warren. "Would you like my booklet?" I said to people and before long it seemed that everybody was busy reading a copy of the booklet.

"Ere, ere, it's good this" said one of rugby players. "I can understand this", said another. "Ere, have this guy's booklet, he wrote it himself" (it was too complicated to explain that my name wasn't Norman Warren).

Amongst all the joking and humour an enormous hulk of a rugby player lowered his head to my ear.

"Here", he said earnestly. "Can this Jesus of yours help me with my marriage?"

Suddenly it was holy ground. No messing around, this was serious business and I hope I gave the answer he was seeking. I prayed for him before we parted company, his eyes moistened

* Journey Into Life, Norman Warren, David C Cook

afterwards and he punched me on the arm as a way of thanking me.

On leaving the pub a car drew up, a good looking couple were inside. The driver was a guy in his thirties.

"Remember me?" I couldn't place him but he went on to say that he was reading his newspaper in a roadside caravan snack bar at Caple Curig the day before and had overheard me talking to the tea ladies about Jesus. Clearly he had been thinking deeply about what he had heard and now wanted to know more.

"I've just got one question to ask you" he said leaning out of the window of his car "How do I?"……. he paused to try to word the question properly.

"How do I get born again?"

I gave a simple Gospel explanation and told him the prayer he needed to pray. However, before I could offer to pray for him, he thanked me profusely and sped off. Our job is to love everyone, fear no one and leave the rest to the Holy Spirit.

The power of your own story

When out in a pub or cafe or even on the streets, I try to share my story of how I met Jesus as soon as possible in the conversation. Most people are bored or even perhaps lonely in pubs and enjoy hearing about somebody's life. I relax when I start to tell my story. Indeed it is often easier just to recall the story of your past life than to try to give a complicated explanation of the Gospel. If we are honest, most of us like talking about ourselves. People also start to identify with parts of your story. When I have, for example talked about being a wimp at school and being the last to be picked at football, people start nodding and begin recalling their school days. As you relax, people relax and when humour flows people begin to enjoy themselves.

But what if my story is boring? Well, no story of meeting Jesus is boring. I have the most 'boring' story perhaps of any. I came to Jesus as soon as I heard about Him. I heard someone say, "I was a terrible womaniser, a bank robber, a street fighter, a drug addict, a drunkard, a gambler, a terrorist ... and at the age of six I found Jesus." I often say that sort of thing to make people laugh, however it is true that at the age of six my mum led me in a prayer to give my life to Jesus. It's the perfect story. In a perfect world everyone would receive Jesus at the earliest opportunity. The miracle isn't that we prayed a prayer to receive Jesus; the miracle is that our lives are different as a result of praying that prayer.

I often encourage people to tell others about their past life, i.e. to recall the part of their life before they met Jesus. Sometimes this story can be very ordinary. This can be actually a helpful factor. It is ok to say "I was a kind of a nice guy before I met Jesus; I never took drugs and things." Most ordinary people can identify with this. They also may not have been in trouble with the police or may never have taken drugs. They may be "Mr and Mrs Ordinary" as well and can identify with you and may respect you for being 'a nice guy'. Some people's response to those who have had a very colourful or broken past life is to say "Oh, they were messed up, they needed Jesus but I'm ok, I'm not messed up". Respectable people need Jesus as well and may identify more with the past life of a respectable person than of those with a messed up background.

But what if you have been messed up by the way life has treated you? Maybe your parents split up, you felt insecure or rejected, you took to drink, you slept around to try to find love, etc. If that is your story, tell people! They need to hear because they may well be going through the very same struggles in their own life.

Some people think that such stories from our past life glorify 'sin'. If it's 'bad', it's seen as a 'good story'. The important thing is whether or not we want to glorify Jesus. Paint a black picture and put one white dot in the middle and most people will tell you that they see a white spot, not a black picture. In the same way a black story is fine, even helpful, provided you major on 'the white dot', provided your main desire is talk about your eventual meeting with Jesus.

Many young Christians often centre, on 'feeling' the presence of the Holy Spirit at a Christian event. Talking about a personal encounter about Jesus is what excites people and I always encourage Christians to highlight the time when they knew that Jesus had touched them in a big way.

Some say that there is little talk about sin and repentance today. Whilst this may be true, we do live in an 'experienced-based' culture and the peace, joy or love that we have felt from God can be appealing today in a culture that often is looking for substitutes for those very feelings. Many people know that the chemicals found in drugs and drink don't give the long-term peace or joy that they look for. I've seen people nod their heads when I've said that relying on human beings to give you love is risky. Humans can let you down! People need a personal encounter with the living God. That is their deepest need! Our experience of meeting God should therefore be one of the most important parts of our story.

However, the most important part of our message is the message of the cross. The truth is; people are carrying around with them a lot of guilt. So many people tell me that they don't like themselves very much. The message of Jesus dying for us on the cross to take away our guilt should always be the central part of our story.

Some people are good at telling the 'before' part of their story, they even do a good job of recounting their decision to follow Jesus. They also get very excited about recounting their first encounter with the Holy Spirit. However, in mid-flight often they will suddenly shut up, finishing with a statement like; "and now my life has changed". When people have done this in a school assembly setting I have often been seen gesticulating to them at the side of the stage urging them to say how their 'life has changed'. The fact is that for many of us, we are not sure how our life has changed. We are not that good at looking at ourselves in that way. I often suggest that people take time to look at how they have become different as a result of receiving Jesus. It seems to me that there are four areas in which our lives can be changed when we meet Jesus.

The first area to be changed concerns **how we are at home**, the real us, the bit our wives, children, parents see. The way we are when we feel that we are 'off duty'. The 'us' that is often hidden from the outside world. Would people still respect us if they knew the real us? I often tell people that at home I can be selfish, miserable, uptight, worried, stressed out, impatient, etc. I can say unkind things, I am not always reliable. I then turn to Galatians Chapter 5 v22 where it talks about fruit of the Spirit. I can then show them from the Bible how the Holy Spirit produces the opposite of our bad qualities. Having Jesus in your life is creating love instead of selfishness, joy instead of being miserable or critical. Peace instead of being uptight, stressed out, etc.

The beauty about being open with your own failings is that people can identify with you because their human nature may be similar to yours. As you have been straight with them it can

help them to become straight with you about the real 'them'.
Indeed, they often end up also confessing their failings to you.
When people hate their sin and want to get their lives right with
God, that's when the good 'old fashioned' word 'repentance'
kicks in. The word repentance means 'rethink'. When a person
desperately wants to do a 'u-turn' in their life you know that the
Holy Spirit is at work. Most people would agree that human
nature is polluted and needs to be renewed. One of my
favourite statements was spoken by Winston Churchill when he
said "The heart of the problem is the problem of the heart."

The verses that I often show to people are John Chapter 3
verse 3-8 which speaks of being born-again and 2 Corinthians
Chapter 5 verse 17 which speaks of becoming a brand new
person, a new creation. People need a new heart. God creates
a total newness in our attitudes at home. I know my failings
in my human nature but I also know that I would be far worse
without Jesus. Anyone who is excited about Jesus will also show
love, joy and peace in their life and often, you will also see it in
their eyes. I have seen the twinkle in the eye of many a Christian;
innocent clean eyes reflecting the purity of Jesus within. The
face of some Christians radiate with joy. I used to play a game as
a child, 'spot the Christian'. Nine out of ten times I got it right.

Another major area in which your life may have been changed
is in **the area of the supernatural.** Many of us have great stories
of Jesus healing today.

When carrying the cross in Sri Lanka I would walk with Debbie, my wife who would often walk slightly ahead singing praise songs. I would be behind carrying the cross, sometimes joining in the singing when it was not too hot to sap all my strength.

As we passed a small house people began running towards us, beckoning us to visit them. It soon became clear that they wanted us to pray for the father of the house, who was slumped in a wheelchair. Debbie carried on singing her worship songs while my good friend 'big Dave' and our missionary friends, 'Thomas and Colleen' gathered around the man to pray. Jesus was there! I could feel Him so strongly! The man's left arm started shaking, then his left leg; eventually he lifted his left arm in the air. His family gasped! I was a little slow on the uptake not realising that their joy was based on their awareness that a stroke had left the man paralysed all down his left side.

To everyone's amazement he proceeded to stand up and walk several yards before returning to his wheelchair. He was a Catholic and he was trying to say "Hallelujah" but the stroke had also affected his speech. We prayed some more and his speech suddenly became clear "Hallelujah" he said over and over again. It was like a scene out of the New Testament. I'd never seen anything like it!

On that same trip a man pushing a bike came over to us. He indicated from the cross roughly tattooed on his arm that he was also a believer. His eyes looked wild and scary but it was

obvious from his gestures that he wanted us to pray for him.
Debbie, discerning that there seemed to be a spiritual battle
erupting started to pray for him to be set free. The man's head
started shaking like a pneumatic drill. His head was shaking so
badly that I thought it would collide with the wing mirror of a
passing lorry. We kept on praying, not totally certain of what
was happening but knew something powerful was going on.
Gradually the shaking stopped and his eyes appeared totally
different. Gone was the scary look and instead, love shone in his
eyes. He seemed happy, very happy and rolled his head the way
Sri Lankan's do, thanking us in his own language. To this day I
am not still completely sure what went on but all I know was that
he came to us in a mess but Jesus appeared to totally set him
free. That's our supernatural Jesus for you!

Some of us have great stories of how God has guided us. I
remember the first time I experienced hearing the voice of God.
I had met a Christian woman in the street whilst selling Christian
magazines called 'Buzz'. I was only eighteen years old at the
time and someone had suggested that this was a great way of
'spreading the Word'. The magazine was about the Jesus people
in America, about hippies and musicians who had met Jesus. It
was well produced, with psychedelic graphics. "Do you want a
Buzz?" I'd say to unsuspecting shoppers.

On this day I met 'Paula' (not her real name). She was a
Christian and had just moved to a village near to our town. She

didn't know any other Christians but gave me her address. The next day I sat out in the garden reading one of Arthur Blessitt's earlier books 'Tell the World'. What an exciting book! It drove on at an unrelenting pace about witnessing everywhere, at boxing matches, on aeroplanes, in nightclubs, in parks, on the streets, etc. Each chapter fired me up but over and above the words of Arthur Blessitt's book came a voice inside me calmly insisting that I should go and visit the woman that I had met the day before.

For a time Arthur Blessitt's book won the day and I told the Lord I would go after I had read the next chapter. However, I just couldn't go on reading. Eventually, I gave in and began driving my motorbike over to the village where 'Paula' lived. On finding her house, she opened the door, saw me and burst into tears (some may say that is the normal effect I have on women!) She began, through her sobs, to tell me that she suffered from depression and was in a suicidal state and only an hour ago she had been imploring the Lord to send me over to find her (the very time I was hearing that voice). Although I was a student social worker at the time I had really no idea how to help her and in the end I stuck her on the back of my motorbike and took her to stay with Ray and Val, the youth leaders at my church until they could get psychiatric help for her. She didn't commit suicide that day and is, I believe alive today thanks to God's still, small voice.

A great Cornish Christian recalls an incident when a small

voice told him to stop his car and call on a person in a caravan at the side of the road. It was night time, raining hard and he thought better of it. However, the next day he found out that the person in the caravan had committed suicide that night. Whenever he recalls that story he implores his fellow Christians to obey that small, insistent voice of God's supernatural Holy Spirit.

The secret of some of the most exciting God-encounters that I have had in my life, has been when I have acted on that small, still, inner voice that calmly directs me to do something.

On one occasion I was approached by an addict in Amsterdam. The little voice of God told me "pray over that man". I resisted the idea feeling that I couldn't just stop a man and start praying over him. However, that's exactly what the Holy Spirit wanted me to do. I gave him a Christian leaflet instead. My friend congratulated me for doing that but I felt so bad that I failed God. God had told me to pray over him and I asked God for a second chance. When I saw the man again I sat next to him, laid my hands on his sweaty head and prayed in tongues over him. What came out of my mouth was the tongue of a mother lamenting over her beloved son. It was totally supernatural.

I was walking past a woman and her young son on a train in New Zealand when I had a clear prompt from God to pray over her. I introduced myself and explained what God had asked me to do. She was shocked and, lowering her voice she confided with me that she been away from God for years. She had got into drugs and many different relationships, and pointing over towards her young son, added that she had got herself pregnant in the process. However, she had just decided to try to sort out her life. Her brother was a born again Christian and she was now on her way back to meet him again, hoping that he would be able to help her. I pointed out that God clearly must love her and that is why I had been prompted to pray for her. She agreed, we bowed our heads and I believe that the dear woman made a big step back to God.

Many of our stories demonstrate God's supernatural provision for us. When I first left social work to 'live by faith' I experienced often God's provision. My first wife was Swiss and when I felt the Lord's calling to work full-time for Him, I left social work and we would work in Swiss restaurants or fruit farms in the summer to gain sufficient funds to return to the UK, hoping that we would have enough to see us through the winter months. One year we were pleased to have managed to save a £1000 during our summer's work. The day we were to leave for the UK a Christian farmer pressed into our hands a wad of Swiss bank notes. On counting it out, we realised he had given us a further £1000.

In the initial years of 'working for God' I lived under, what might be described as, 'a spirit of frugality'. Money was extremely tight and we therefore lived as simply as we could in order that we could make ends meet. I had got it into my head that I should give a Gospel booklet to every house in my estate and quickly set about writing one. The printing costs turned out to be £40, a significant amount in the early 1980's. To my amazement, as soon as I paid the bill, a tax rebate arrived for £40 exactly. I love these stories.

While carrying the cross in Sri Lanka Debbie hurt her knee. No sooner had she done this, a little voice inside urged her to walk one step further. As she did that a man appeared from the crowd and insisted we stay at his father's ex-colonial mansion. It turned out that his brother had just become a born-again Christian and he wanted to know how he also could be born again. God provided us with an empty mansion for us to stay in that night and he got to hear how to be born-again.

Many days later on the Sri Lanka walk my wife began to be seriously ill. She had an allergic reaction to mosquito bites, her legs were covered with blisters. We tried to get local medical help but she wasn't coping at all well. As we were walking along a lonely jungle road, a suave Sri Lankan man emerged from his pickup truck. He introduced himself as Brian. He had seen the cross being carried and "was curious". There was a distinct Englishness in the way he pronounced "curious" and it transpired that he had worked as a policeman in Streatham, London for many years. He turned to my wife and said "You're ill, I can tell!" He said that he had friends down the road who could speak English and that he would go ahead and arrange for us to stay with them.

We settled down with his friends, who welcomed us immediately. Some Sri Lankan women arrived. They used to be Buddhist but Jesus had appeared to them while they were meditating and they were now followers of Jesus. I was so enthralled by their story that I hadn't realised that Deb was in her bedroom going downhill rapidly. She was obviously in a high fever and could only mumble something about going to a western hotel.

Brian, a Seventh Day Adventist saved the day again. He had felt compelled to return to see us and as soon as he arrived insisted that he transport us to the Seventh Day Adventist Hospital over the pass in the city of Kandy. The western style hospital took charge of Debbie and we were housed in the air conditioned 'luxury' suite. (I think Brian had something to do with that.) The hospital saved Deb's life. Debbie's allergy had started to create anaphylactic shock which, if the swelling had got to her throat, would have killed her. (She now travels with an Epi-Pen to prevent such incidents occurring.)

During the night Christian nurses would appear like angels and pray over her, stroke her hair and tell her that she was beautiful. Deb usually gets quite tearful when she recounts this story of how God provided for us in a wonderful way.

People love these stories about God's supernatural healings

or provision. The magazines and television are full of the supernatural. Let's talk of our supernatural Jesus as part of our testimony.

Another powerful part of our story is how Jesus has affected our **moral conscience**. Even before we give our lives to Jesus our conscience can be very much alive and kicks in big time when we offend. At worst, we hate ourselves and feel full of shame. At best we all know that 'yukky' feeling when we do wrong.

Many young people tell me that they feel bad about sleeping around even though our culture says it's fine to do it. Promiscuity, dishonesty, drug and drink abuse often make people feel guilty or ashamed inside. People who use or abuse others rarely look happy. In fact, they usually carry a darkness and hardness in their face.

To be set free and cleansed from dirty or dishonest living is an incredibly powerful part of our story. I am amazed when I hear some of my Christian friends recount what they used to be like before they met Jesus. When they tell their story it's hard to believe that they are talking about the same person.

One of my friends used to be drunk so badly that he wouldn't even remember being banned from the local pubs. My good mate, Dave, is one of the most warmest and affable men you could ever meet. Yet before he met Jesus he was so full of anger he would use his job as a 'bouncer' on the doors of the nightclub to legitimise his desire to hurt people. It's just so hard to imagine that this was the old Dave. Jesus changes us big time!

Finally, **Jesus changes people spiritually**, he gives us spiritual certainties. In a world of spiritual uncertainties and confusion, this is perhaps the most powerful part of our story. Jesus said that He had come to give sight to the blind and to show those who thought they could see, that they were, in fact, spiritually blind.

Prior to becoming a Christian you may have had all sorts of weird and wonderful spiritual beliefs but may have been very confused as to what is truth. You may have experienced the fear often associated with looking into the occult, or even feel trapped by the unyielding control system of a cult ('Christian' or otherwise). Maybe the beliefs associated with the religion with which you were raised have left you full of uncertainties.

To be able to say with absolute authority and absolute sincerity that you now know God personally is incredible. To add to that statement that you both love God and hear His gentle voice revealing His will for you, is even more amazing. To say that you believe that Jesus is the Son of God and that He was raised on the third day is so powerful. The assurance that Jesus gives; that you have forgiveness of sins and know that you are going to heaven is unique to our faith. All this can be very impressive to an individual whose search for reality has only left them confused and full of questions. Some accuse Christians of narrow-minded dogmatism but to be certain of spiritual truths in an uncertain world can be very attractive, appealing and convincing to those who are hungry for the truth.

Something happens when you pray that doesn't when you don't

I know no other way than to prepare myself to share Jesus on the streets than to pray, pray and pray. I have heard it said that no man is greater than his prayer life. Others have said that "prayer is the most powerful form of energy that we can generate". John Wesley is quoted as saying "Prayer changed the profile of England, far more than my preaching."

We need to work hard at prayer and then walk out of the door and allow God to help us pick up the results of our prayer! After weeks of witnessing with little prayer and little results, I decided to change my priorities. I decided to spend at least an hour walking up and down St Mark's Church, Kennington, London pouring my heart out before God. As I left the church that morning I was bubbling over with excitement from the Lord. A young couple were sitting over on the church steps. Within a miraculously short time they were praying to accept Jesus.

I guess I am not everybody's 'cup of tea' in a prayer meeting. I get too passionate about things and end up 'rabbiting on' all around the houses, praying for everyone and everything. Then just when I take a breath and people think that they can get a word in edgeways, off I go again, this time in tongues. I have tried 'waiting on the Lord' and 'resting in Jesus'. I just end up nodding off. I have only two speeds, 'fast forward' or 'asleep'.

That funny language stuff

One evening in London I was struggling to cope with a dry prayer meeting and decided to go out in the streets for some air.

"Ere do you do that funny language stuff?"

Turning around I saw a face I recognised. Behind me was standing a skinhead that I'd seen before when I had preached on his bus. His face had an evil darkness about it and he had sworn at me at that time, trying to shut me up. However now, here he was asking if I spoke in tongues.

"How do you know about speaking in tongues?" I asked.

"Well, when I was in prison, I read this book, didn't I, about this gangster bloke who ended up meeting Jesus and speaking in tongues and that."

"Nicky Cruz ... Run Baby Run* ?" I suggested. He seemed pleased that I knew what he was talking about.

"Go on then!" he urged, "Go on, do it!"

"Do what?"

"Do that speaking in tongues thing!"

"I'm not into party tricks and to be honest I'm not sure that I could do that speaking in tongues thing to order."

In the end I decided to do a deal with him "Tell you what

* Run Baby Run, Nicky Cruz, Hodder & Stoughton

mate, if you let me pray for you in English to start with, then, if I start speaking in tongues afterwards you'll have your speaking in tongues."

That's exactly what happened. Standing outside the local pub, the young skinhead and a couple of his mates bowed their head while I prayed for them. Sure enough, before long I was praying away in tongues. This went on for quite a time but after a while I suddenly had the thought, "I know what's happened, while I've had my eyes shut they've nipped into the pub, leaving me standing outside, hand raised in the air, babbling away in the funny language stuff."

I sneaked a quick look. To my surprise, there they were, heads still bowed. Eventually I finished and looked up. "Right" they said awkwardly "Right ... erm ... thanks ... yeah ... right ..." Their words drifted to nothing as they kind of shuffled off very subdued. I rejoined the prayer meeting bemused at what had just happened.

"Hey Paul!" The same skinhead addressed my pastor a few weeks later. "You know that skinny preacher bloke with long hair …. You know ... with a moustache."

"Aye……. you mean Lindsay?" Paul Shepherd replied.

"Yeah **Lindsay**, whatever ... well we used to think he was a right xxxx nutter but now we don't 'cause he did that tongues thing over us and we ... well we ... well while he was doing it we had this funny feeling come over us and we reckon it was God ...

so we don't think he's a nutter no more."

I cannot say that I had felt the Holy Spirit when I had prayed over them but something had seemed to change in these boys and I believe it was God who touched them.

Prayer changes things

One of Arthur Blessitt's Jesus stickers used to say "Prayer changes things". I've heard it said that if we give God space to move our circumstances change. As we spend time in prayer and we take on the heart of God, so we change. As we pray our security and authority in God is built up. This leads to the activity of the devil being forced to change. Finally, I know that when we are alone with God a love, joy and peace begins to radiate from us. When people see God in us something stirs in them and so they end up changing themselves. How often do you hear people say "I saw that Christians had something that I hadn't got and I wanted what they had."

I have found that the time spent in prayer before going out to share Jesus is worth every minute. I think I recall Jackie Pullinger saying in her book "Chasing the Dragon* " that she noticed the difference in what happened on the streets when she spent twenty minutes praying in tongues beforehand. Arthur Blessitt recalls trying to start his first church in a hard industrial town. He tried witnessing and witnessing to people, no one wanted to know. Eventually he spent a night in prayer. The next day he

* Chasing the Dragon, Jackie Pullinger, Hodder & Stoughton

had his first convert, a young man ready to accept Jesus. The saying I love is that "Things happen when you pray, that don't when you don't."

Night-time preparation

In Bangladesh Dave and I had a strange experience while we were trying to get to sleep one night.

"Are you awake Linds?"

"I am now", I replied to Dave.

"I feel we've got to pray" continued Dave out of the pitch darkness.

The electricity had gone off, no A/C, no fan, just intense heat. It was 3am. We were due to start carrying the cross in Muslim Bangladesh the following morning.

On getting up from my bed I found myself praying immediately in tongues and spinning around in the dark as I did so. This lasted for an hour and then suddenly stopped. I know people view me as a mad extrovert but I really do not court crazy behaviour. However, this unusual behaviour was not man-ordained; the Holy Spirit had hold of me and was praying through me. At the same time Dave felt lead to reach out for his notepad and began scribbling down whatever God gave him in the dark. Suddenly, as if God had switched a switch, we stopped and fell to sleep.

In the morning, Dave looked down at his notepad, his writing was both legible and lucid, prophesy after prophesy. God was spiritually preparing us for the task ahead. I recall reading about an Eastern European Christian who would spin around in circles praising God at the top of his voice in his prison cell whenever he heard a Christian being tortured in the cell beneath his. When challenged about his bizarre behaviour he maintained that he believed that his specific manner of praising was a form of intense warfare combating the darkness and evil that was assailing his Christian brother in the torture cell beneath him.

A movement of prayer

Just before starting the walk with the cross in Sri Lanka I was filled with fear during the night, I was plagued with thoughts that I was leading my wife into great danger. The evil could be felt. In the morning it transpired that my wife and my friend, Dave, had also had experienced a disturbed, anxiety–filled night.

"Let's start praising!" Deb said, reaching for her guitar. As soon as we began singing praise songs the fear that had gripped us left instantly. A short time later I thudded the cross down on my shoulder to begin our walk in Sri Lanka and the joy of God 'flooded my soul'.

The very first person we met was an old man with pebble glasses, pushing a bike. We told him that we were praying for the Holy Spirit to be outpoured in Sri Lanka. "You must join us," he urged. "There are hundreds that gather to pray every week in

Colombo for the Holy Spirit to be outpoured". We couldn't join him at his meetings but knew that we were part of something bigger than we realised. Prayer, praise and power are effective bed mates!

When Jesus turns up

I know that there were a couple of occasions during my time preaching on London's tube train platforms, when, halfway through my preaching, the Spirit was suddenly there in power. It was supernatural! On both times, it forced me to stop preaching. All I could say to the public was "He is here, can't you feel Him, can't you feel Him?" I remember thinking that revival had broken out at the time. I was a little confused that when the tube train arrived everybody just got into the train. However, on both occasions, somebody came up to me shaking my hand vigorously saying "I was praying for you with all my heart while you were preaching." It's a cocktail that's explosive, get the prayer warriors and the preachers working together and things happen. We are a body and different parts have different functions. The heavy duty prayer guys needs to work in unison with the evangelistic types.

Prayer Walking

I joined a prayer walk from London to Berlin in 1992. That one took five weeks. Next year a further walk took place, this time with many Germans in the team. We walked from Berlin to Moscow. That took three months. Ostensibly, these were reconciliation walks, initially with British Christians asking the Germans for forgiveness for their part in the war. I was privileged to hear my old mate Matt McCarthy, a former bomber pilot, speaking over the loud speaker system to over 80,000 German Christians during their march for Jesus.

"I have been to Berlin three times already; the first times it was to drop bombs on your women and children."

You could have heard a pin drop!

"Since then I have become a Christian and I asked God for the opportunity to ask for your forgiveness, will you forgive me?"

A German pastor came onto the stage, got on his knees and kissed Matt's feet saying, "We forgive you!" Not many dry eyes that day!

German Christians asked the same thing when we walked from Berlin to Moscow the next year. Again, many tears and many hugs. Reconciliation! This type of thing is not strictly street outreach but can pave the way spiritually for exciting things to happen on the streets.

Andrew Chapel, a local pastor and an advocate of prayer walking and spiritual warfare, uses an illustration of a town near to me in Cornwall. The Christians in St Ives spent weeks prayer walking around one particular housing estate. They followed this with a successful door-to-door visitation. They attempted to do this again in a neighbouring estate but without the prayer preparation. However this time, they found an opposite response, people were markedly closed to the Gospel. Prayer changes things!

Arthur Blessitt signs all his letters with Luke Chapter 18 v 1 which in my Living Bible reads "One day Jesus told his disciples a story to illustrate their need for constant prayer and to show them that they must keep praying until the answer comes." I have seen God come in power on these prayer walks. During the walk to Moscow a priest turned up from nowhere and led us through the border into Belarus. The guards all knew him and with almost no formalities waved us through, support vehicles included. Once through the border he disappeared again. In normal circumstances, it could often take days to get through the borders at that time.

Getting into Russia itself was even more spectacular! We had been warned by the Russian authorities not to come. A potential civil war was brewing, with an attempted coup being staged against President Yeltsin. The authorities stressed that they could not give us any security and we were asked to count the cost if we decided to go forward towards Moscow.

Just a short distance from the Russian border we formed ourselves into a long line, with a view to marching together in pairs. I was up the front with the cross along side a French guy who also carried a cross. He spoke little English and we couldn't communicate too well, not that I felt like doing too much talking, my thoughts were about the danger ahead. Fear can grip you at times like this. Was I ready to live or, if necessary, die for Jesus? I remember being very quiet as we set off towards the Russian border. Would civil war breakout? We were walking straight for it. Would I end up getting a bullet in my head? "Hopefully the cross will protect me" I mused. It seems a bit overdramatic now but it was very real at the time. I have been through a few 'garden of Gethsemane' experiences while carrying the cross, where I felt God was asking me to be prepared to give my life for Him. If bravery means 'no fear', then I'm not brave at all.

Jesus said "If any of you wants to be my follower, you must turn from your selfish ways, take up your cross, and follow me. If you try to hang onto your life, you will lose it. But if you give up your life for my sake, you will save it," (Mark ch.8 verses 34 to 36) Both in Sri Lanka and Bangladesh Christians have sought to dissuade us from walking, saying we would put our lives in danger. It is a battle you have to go through! This was the first time I'd faced danger on this level and I was wrapped up with fear. How I feel for soldiers waiting in their landing crafts to face machine gun fire as soon as their boat hits the beach. Armchair Christianity knows little fear but on this occasion this was for real and I was scared!

However, as our party of some sixty or so prayer walkers made its way beside the miles of trucks waiting to enter Russia, a power built up within us that seemed to force us on. Everyone was praying! I was praying constantly under my breath in tongues. It was as if there was a powerful steam train behind us pushing us towards the border crossing. I felt as if we were unstoppable. Even if a Russian tank had appeared in front us we would have, like an army of ants, marched over it. Such was the power of prayer experienced that morning.

When we reached the border the guards just stepped aside. We weren't even sure that we had crossed the border. Eventually, after a mile or so of what we presumed was no-mans land, we were met by a single man waiting for us by the side of the road. He looked just like a KGB Agent from a James Bond film, trilby hat and grey gabardine coat.

"This was where they arrest us." my good old friend, John Pressdee, muttered under his breath.

"You must be the prayer expedition." the 'KGB Agent' asked. "The authorities in Moscow told me to turn you back. I told them you can come all the way from Moscow to turn them back yourselves if you want, I am going to welcome them, Welcome to Russia!" he beamed. He put his arms open wide to hug and kiss us Russian style. He wasn't a KGB Agent but the local Orthodox priest who immediately found us accommodation. The power of prayer!

Russian bibles

On another occasion, in Eastern Germany, I had seen the power
of prayer. I had been brought up in the days of the cold war
and prayed for Christians who had suffered under Communism.
Pastor Richard Wurmbrandt was one of my heroes. He had
suffered terribly in prison for his faith and on his release into the
West wrote a very powerful book, 'Tortured for Christ'. I had
seen him interviewed on late night television just after he came
to England. I remember being transfixed by the light shining
from his face and this was instrumental in me deciding to follow
Jesus in a serious way. I never ever dreamt that one day I would
get to witness about Jesus in former Communist countries.
While walking through the town of Brandenburg, in the former
East German Republic, I found myself walking past a Russian
army camp. I could see rows of Russian soldiers relaxing on
their parade ground. My heart started beating very fast. "Here's
my chance to preach to the Russians!" I began preaching my
heart out, I even stood the cross up erect and then proceeded
to mime Jesus dying on the cross. I don't think I was making
a great impression on the soldiers, none of whom could
understand any English. I guess it was inevitable that within a
short time the military police arrived and I was told to move on.
I was a little embarrassed at my antics, feeling certain that I had
made a fool of myself with my over-enthusiasm. However, as we
came by the main entrance, I sought to have a second attempt

to preach, this time to the Russian soldier on guard at the gate. I didn't do too much better on this occasion either but what did happen this time was that his eyes appeared to become fixated on my Bible, "Biblia....Biblia", he started to bark. I guessed that he wanted me to give him my Bible. My Bible was very precious to me and I was reluctant to give it away, especially to a Russian who couldn't speak a word of English. All he could say was, "Biblia" which he repeated over and over again.

"Biblia – English!......I get Biblia – Russian for you!" I shouted, hoping that by shouting he would understand me better. He seemed to understand and a faint smile broke out on his face. The Russians are not always smiley, smiley types. The hardness of their lives under Communism had perhaps driven any openness out of them. However, I have learnt that stony faces can, at times hide a warm heart.

I left the soldier content that I had offered to find him a Russian Bible. However, I immediately begun wondering how on earth I could fulfil my promise. At the end of our walk that day the local pastor told me that he had a couple of Russian Bibles, although one of them was only a children's Bible. "That's fine" I said "can we take them to the camp now?" A noisy old Trabant car appeared. I think they are collector's items now. The pastor and I bounced along the cobbled streets, hardly able to hear ourselves talk. Over and above the growl of the engine, we prayed together two specific prayers. Firstly, that there would be a Russian interpreter at the camp, and secondly, that every soldier would be able to receive a Bible, not just the one at the gate. At the camp entrance a small crowd had gathered. There was an East German policeman, a very dignified Commandant of the camp and a woman. Apparently a car had been left outside the entrance and this had been deemed to be a security risk. The German police were dealing with the matter and the woman was interpreting for the Russian Commandant. I suddenly saw my opportunity here.

"Excuse me." I said "Does anyone here speak English."

"Yes I do!" replied the translator in a strong accent.

"Well.............. I would like to give these Bibles to you! One is for the guard at the gate."

The Bibles were gratefully received and since we had got our first prayer answered we gained courage to push for the answer to our second prayer. We stuck our necks out and went for gold!

"I wonder if we could give a Bible to every soldier in the camp."

The Commandant, on hearing that request, mumbled something in Russian and went back to the guard room, emerging a few minutes later.

"I would like 240 Bibles please," came the reply.

I could hardly believe what had happened. My heart was racing with excitement and with a new zeal welling up inside of me I found myself asking the Commandant if he had ever given his life to Jesus.

"I often think about Jesus during difficult times!" he confessed.

I asked him if he minded me leading him in a short prayer for him to give his life over to Jesus. He nodded and what followed was a beautiful scene. Translated from English to German, from German to Russian and back again, the commandant humbly prayed 'the sinner's prayer' to commit his life to the Lord. It took three times as long as usual, since it had to be translated three times but there was no doubting the sincerity of the prayer.

I understand that the local church sacrificed greatly to purchase all the Bibles and when they were due to be given out formally, in true military style; they were stacked neatly on tables ready to be given out in an orderly fashion. However, when it was stated that the soldiers could now receive their Bible, they broke ranks and just ran to the table frantically grabbing their own copy of the Bible. The local church were then able to hold Bible studies at the camp until the Russian soldiers eventually returned to their home country.

Pray and do

We are encouraged to walk in the Spirit and we may find ourselves closely involved in being part of the answer to our prayers. God takes our praying that seriously. Do we really mean what we pray, to the extent that we will really act on our prayers?

On one of those prayer walks through Europe a local pastor had asked that we refrained from carrying the cross through their town. It might upset either the Catholics or the Protestants (I don't remember which).

I've never really been good at submitting to authority, so wasn't happy at all about this request not to carry the cross. People have called me a 'maverick', 'loose cannon' and the like. A certain brand of Christian always wants to know who is covering me. "It's God that covering me." I reply and then realise from their expression that I haven't given them the right answer. In their book I should have some super Christian telling me what to do and when to do it. I've always maintained that it's usually control freaks who use words like 'maverick' and such like. They have the Kingdom of God all sorted out with shepherds of different ranks telling us lower Christians how to hear from the Spirit. Well I believe Jesus talked about 'the Kingdom of God' not 'the kingdom of man'. God is King. I will do what He says, not what Christian dictators say.

Of course, God wants us to listen to people with a pastor's heart. I am certainly happy to make myself accountable to godly pastors or individuals that will help me hear from God and obey Him. However, I see such pastors more as advisors, not controllers. On the streets it is impossible to operate effectively if you are not listening to the promptings of God's loving Holy Spirit. I could never survive on the streets if I had to rely on checking all the time with the local heavy duty shepherd! Anyway on this occasion I decided to eat humble pie and obey the pastor. I wasn't happy at all! However, I was delighted that my friend, John Pressdee, who was leading the prayer expedition, could not get any peace about leaving the cross behind either. He decided that we must have it with us.

On entering the town the local pastor suggested that my friend, John, should lead us in a prayer outside the railway station. John found himself praying passionately for the youth of the town, which excited the pastor greatly, since John was not to know that usually the youth of the town tended to hang out at the railway station. They weren't hanging out that day at the railway station but, as we found out later, a great many of them were congregated just off the central shopping area. I spied a great horde of them outside a bar, down a side street.

"Oi" I cried, trying to get the attention of the pastor who was in intense discussion at the front of the march.

"Look, young people!" I shouted. The pastor looked at me blankly.

"It's no good praying for young people if we are not prepared to talk to them when we meet them." I started getting a little impatient that he couldn't see the logic of my argument.

My friend, John Pressdee did however see my logic and suggested that we spend a short time with the young people. On venturing down the side street, the cross was held erect. I leapt on a plastic chair outside the bar and began preaching.

"Excuse me everyone, we have walked all the way from Berlin to tell you that Jesus ..." As soon as I mentioned the word 'Jesus' all hell was let loose. The youngsters began shouting and within minutes the landlord of the pub appeared two inches from my face, with his finger pointing telling me that if I didn't shut up he was going to call the police immediately. This really freaked out the pastor who demanded that we beat a hasty retreat. I wasn't going anywhere and dropped to my knees and started to pray. "What is he doing now?" I heard the pastor say, exasperated. Dear John Pressdee, ever the diplomat, suggested that the pastor and anyone else who wanted should carry on prayer walking. He suggested that those who wanted to stay behind should do so. Most of the walkers left, but a small group of us stayed behind and things started happening. Each of us had a small group around us firing questions at us. "What happens when you die?", "Why is God against sex before marriage?" Before long one of my friends came to me with a young lad next to him. "This boy has just prayed to receive Jesus." Prayer was going on all around.

I went into the pub where' Thrash Metal' was being played and within minutes I was talking or, maybe I should say screaming out a conversation with a long-haired guy.

"So how do I receive Jesus?" he shouted.

"Pray this prayer with me" I screamed. I led him in the 'sinner's prayer'. However, as he started praying, for some reason the music suddenly turned off. All you could hear in the bustling pub was the sound of this long-haired guy asking Jesus to "forgive his sins and come into his heart" at the top of his voice. A peace fell, I could feel Jesus strongly, even in that setting, Jesus was there!

What followed next I will never forget. The same landlord, who had earlier threatened to call the police, came over to me. This time his attitude was totally different. "You people can come back anytime. What you've done for my young people is wonderful. You see many of them do not have love in their lives. Their parents have split up and they are looking for love in relationships but are just using each other. They take drugs and get drunk to try to find peace and happiness. What you have done today is truly great, come back anytime."

I couldn't believe what I was hearing from this landlord. He had talked of his customers as <u>his</u> young people. He obviously cared about them and demonstrated an amazing understanding and compassion for them. He had more of a pastor's heart than many a Christian pastor. Oh that we would gain that type of love for the teenagers in our towns!

On leaving the bar, one of the prayer walkers came over to me full of excitement. She couldn't tell me quick enough that she had just seen a vision become reality, right then, in front of her eyes. What had happened was that, prior to coming on the walk she had attended a 'Youth with a Mission' conference. In one of the meetings she had received a vision of the cross being erected and many young people were receiving Jesus. What had happened was just as God had shown her in the vision.

On the way back to the church, I suddenly had a full-on migraine headache, even seeing double. I never usually suffer from migraines and I don't know whether this was just exhaustion or a devilish attack. What I do know was that I had seen the power of prayer; of prayer and action working hand-in-hand. I believe in spiritual warfare and intercession .We need those who will hold up Moses' arms in the midst of the battle.

One of my favourite friends was old Charles Simpson. He walked with us from London to Berlin and then Berlin to Moscow. Finally he walked from Berlin to Paris. He did all this at the young age of 82 years old. "We haven't prayed together recently Lindsay, have we?" he'd say. He spoke like a high-ranking British Army General. "Well Lord," he'd start….. "Thank you for my own chum Lindsay" He would then go off addressing the good lord at some length in his delightful clipped English accent. Sometimes he would wait outside German nightclubs praying for me while I witnessed inside. I remember him coming out with me one night. Eventually, at some unearthly hour Charles asked if it would be alright if he could be excused since "it was getting rather late and he was afraid that he really could do with retiring to his bed if that was alright with me?"

I last talked with Charles on the outskirts of Paris. The dear man completed his walk from Berlin to Paris and went to bed that night and died. On hearing the news of his death I felt the Lord say "Charles has lived walking by the side of the Jordan all his life. It's just that this time he's stayed on my side." Charles always wanted to die with his boots on and so his good friend, Archie lovingly set about dressing his body in his walking gear, boots and all. Charles Simpson, what a prayer warrior! He knew that prayer and witness go hand-in-hand.

CHAPTER 3

LOVE BEYOND WORDS

Meeting Jesus on the streets
Love that breaks barriers
Caring for hurting people
Will we go where Jesus goes?

Meeting Jesus on the streets

I recall hearing that Mother Teresa addressed a reporter who was about to accompany her on the streets of Calcutta. "You will see Jesus today!" she announced to him. After a day of ministering to the sick and dying in the slums and on the streets of Calcutta they returned to her mission. On the way home she quietly asked the reporter "Did you see Jesus today?"

"Then these righteous friends will cry 'Lord when did we ever see you hungry and feed you? Or thirsty and give you something to drink? Or a stranger and give you hospitality? Or naked and give you clothing? When did we ever see you sick and in prison?' And the King will say 'I tell you the truth, when you did it to one of the least of these my brothers and sisters you were doing it to me." (Matthew Chapter 25 v 40)

The smell of body odour was overpowering, as I entered the tube train. I looked to my right and the whole section was jammed with people. The left section, however, was completely empty apart from one dishevelled tramp. His hair and beard was matted, his clothes blackened with grime and the stench emanating from him appeared to have driven his fellow travellers, to the far end of the carriage, giving him ample room to stretch out. It was Mothering Sunday that weekend and I had spent my last bit of cash on a bunch of flowers for my mother. My parents, at that time, lived in Banbury, some 70 miles north of

London and I was going home to see my good ol' mum.
I looked at the dear tramp sitting on his own and wondered what
had brought him to be in that state. Was it alcohol, divorce,
mental illness or maybe a mixture of all three? What was his
childhood like? Did he get brought up in care, having to fight
his way through life? Had he done time in prison? What was
his life like now? Did he sleep rough? Did he have any friends
or family? What did he find the hardest to bear.......the cold
at night, the hunger or that awful loneliness? I stood at the
entrance of the carriage wondering whether to join the other
travellers in their section or to sit next to the tramp.
"Give him your flowers!" I felt the Holy Spirit prompting.
"But I haven't any money to buy any more and it's Mothering
Sunday" I argued. A good way of knowing if God is guiding you
is to ask yourself firstly, is the loving thought that has just popped
into your mind the sort of thing that Jesus would say? Secondly,
am I arguing with that thought because it goes against my fearful
or selfish human nature?
"But people don't usually give flowers to tramps." I whimpered
back to God. We should never take a lead from what people
usually do or don't do. Our lead should always come from 'What
would Jesus do?' and he would definitely give flowers to a lonely
tramp.
"When was the last time someone gave you flowers mate?" I
said, sitting next to the old guy.

"No one's ever given me flowers son!" He answered in a broad Glaswegian accent. I had worked in a children's home in Scotland for a few months before doing my social work training and loved the Glaswegian accent. In fact, in the early weeks in the children's home, the kids' accents were so broad I could barely make out what they were saying to me. I used to be known as 'big Lindsay' by all the kids. That wasn't because I was big, in fact I'm anything but big but it was because there was another boy, a six year old, who was known as 'wee Lindsay'. The children's home was for children who were deemed 'maladjusted'. Because their background was so disturbed they had started showing very strange and antisocial behaviour. Often tables, staff and kids alike would go flying as one of them would lose their temper over the slightest provocation. Some were children of alcoholics and prostitutes and would have witnessed things that a child should not have to witness. My time at the home was, for me, a baptism of fire and I would often find myself ducking punches and trying to avoid being bitten. One boy threw half a house brick at me. This, normally speaking, wouldn't have worried me but on this occasion it hit me, almost breaking my arm. Despite these episodes I grew to love the children and now, some forty years later, still remember their names. I wonder whatever happened to them. In fact the tramp sitting next to me could well have had an upbringing similar to one of these youngsters.

"Here, have these." I said thrusting the flowers into the tramp's hands. "They are a present from Jesus." I added and began to laugh. The tramp also saw the funny side of it. Just then the tube train stopped in the middle of the tunnel. On these occasions I would usually spring to my feet and do a short gospel preach while everything was deathly quiet. I decided to preach. As soon as I finished my address the train engine started off and we went into the station. "Can I do anything else for you?" I asked as we shuffled off the train.

"Wouldn't mind a little cash for a bite to eat." he mumbled.
"I've no money pal, honest, it all went on the flowers." I replied. No sooner as I had said that, a Caribbean lady thanked me profusely for preaching, placing money into my hand. This was followed closely by a very dignified, well-spoken lady who asked me a profound question. Nodding towards the tramp she asked, "Is this man a relative of yours?" I thought for a moment and replied "Yes, very much so, we've got the same dad."
"I thought so!" she countered whilst thrusting more money into my hand. I was not only able to buy the tramp some food but there was just enough to buy some flowers for Mothering Sunday, that's our Father God for you!

The touch of Jesus

It looked like the baby was dead. It certainly looked very lifeless. The mother's face captured the pain and despair of life on the streets of the sprawling city of Chittagong, Bangladesh. She was clutching her baby slumped down by a pillar on the top of some steps. Despite the many beggars seeking to home in on us two westerners, Debbie's eyes were on this woman. Her heart went out to her but there was no way that she could get to her without having to cross an open sewer. There was nothing for it, she clasped her hand over her nose and mouth and gingerly navigated the sewer to make her way across the steps. The woman looked up with empty, sad eyes and then looked down to her baby. Debbie removed the cotton scarf, that Asian woman wear, from around her neck. She wrapped it around the mother and child and began to pray. The woman began to cry and so did Deb. Meanwhile a large crowd had gathered. Westerners are not that common a sight in Chittagong. Even at the best of times we were a novelty, to see a western woman cuddling and praying over a Bengali beggar drew a lot of attention. Normally I'd be itching to preach to the crowd but my translator was not with me and apart from this everyone's eyes were on Deb. Here was Jesus' love being shown without words. Deb and I left the steps giving out biscuits to the many beggars as we went. Returning a short while later we found that most of the beggars had now gone. However, our lady with the baby was still there, but this time, her face was radiant. The baby was suckling on her mum, who was excitedly pointing heavenwards. We still don't know exactly what had transpired but the woman clearly wanted to give God the glory with her finger directing her praises to God.

On another occasion in Chittagong we prayed for an old beggar lady who knew no English but our translator asked if we could pray for her. As we began to pray we felt the Holy Spirit come upon us. More amazingly, to our utter surprise, so could she! The old lady knew nothing about the Holy Spirit. We were probably the first Christians she'd ever met. However, as we prayed, her head shot back, her hands raised in the air and she gasped two or three times in apparent ecstasy. I had never seen anything like it. We had not explained the gospel or said too much at all and yet here was Jesus touching her.

Love that breaks barriers

"Can you lend me 50p towards buying a condom", one prostitute asked me on one of my first days at Kings Cross." (The area around the railway station was known for drugs and prostitution.) My short time at Bible College had not educated me on the ethics of whether I, as a Christian, should give the prostitute 50p towards buying a condom. Although not from a street background, I wore my hair long and unkempt at the time. Together with a droopy moustache, worn out biker's jacket, grubby jeans and an emaciated frame (I was very skinny in those days), I was often mistaken for a drug pusher. "I've got something better than what you've got!" I'd tell drug pushers.

I'd string them along a bit before telling them what I was really pushing. One guy thought that 'Jesus' was a slang name for some new super drug!

The police used CCTV around that Kings cross area and my antics must have looked very suspicious on camera as I, with my scruffy 'drug pusher looks' approached real drug users and prostitutes. How were they to know that I was pushing Jesus and not drugs? Trying to persuade the police that I was legitimate wasn't always easy. It was often only when I actually began asking them personally about their own relationship with Jesus that they would begin to take me seriously. I remember being approached by one policeman while I was preaching. I thought I was going to be in trouble, "Keep going mate," he whispered." If they put into practice what you're preaching about, it would certainly make our job a darn sight easier "

I often felt totally out of my depth in those first days. I would meet all sorts of people and rarely felt prepared for the challenges that I experienced. Sometimes people felt very threatened by me. Looking back, I can kind of see why. I hardly looked a picture of respectability and here I was challenging members of the public (in a city where few even look at each other let alone talk to each other) about such highly charged matters as their relationship with God! No wonder I was a threat! On occasions I would clearly stir up strong emotions in some people. Certain Gay people for instance sometimes seemed to feel greatly threatened by my talk of the love of Jesus and would respond aggressively, 'firing all guns'. They wouldn't even let me get a word in edgeways. Other gay guys were not so quick to tell me that they were homosexual. They were the gentle, sensitive individuals who would usually tell me that they "felt sure that I would reject them if I knew about them". I would usually guess what they were trying to tell me and would seek to make it easy for them to confide in me. "Is this a sexual matter?" I might enquire quietly and they would nod. My starting point has always been that "God loved the world so much". I believe He loves the Muslim world, the Hindu world, etc. He also must love those who are ardent atheists, feminists, homosexuals or any other group who may take issue with certain teachings in the Bible. If God loves them, so should we! I sought to love all people but that, of course didn't mean that they necessarily wanted to receive that love. Some preferred to 'shoot me down' before even getting to know me.

However, there were those from the gay community who wanted to talk. Whether it was discussing spiritual issues or intimate issues of sexuality, I tried to be sensitive. "There is no such thing as homosexuality." advised one Christian worker, who specialised in reaching out to the gay community. "There are only people with complex psycho-sexual issues" he added. I was anxious to understand. "It's not the sex I'm after" admitted one homosexual, "it's the love."

It's not easy to help the person who has adopted a battleship position against you. They don't want your help. However, there are those who really appreciate that you are trying to understand who they are and can sense that you genuinely want to help them know Jesus as a personal friend. I do believe that it is our role to reach out to every type of person with the love of Jesus.

A few years ago I was passing a young man who was racing to catch a train. To my surprise I felt a strong urge to talk to him about God. In order to stop him in his tracks I thrust one of my Christian leaflets in his hand. "This is the story of how I met Jesus." I told him. He went deathly pale. I wondered what I had said wrong.

"Why did you talk to me?" he asked.

"No idea ... I just get these thoughts come into my mind sometimes! I know that God wants me to talk to you." I replied. He looked even more shaken!

"I used to be a Christian but I've gone far from God and got involved in a homosexual relationship. I felt so guilty and asked God for a sign this morning to show me that He was real. Well the young man got his sign perhaps sooner than expected! We prayed together on the train platform. He shook my hand warmly as he got on the train.

The older I get, the more I realise how much I need to learn. Often my answer to more and more issues is that I just don't know the answer! What I do believe, is that God loves people!

I may not understand every person's beliefs or orientation, but I believe God does. The important thing is to seek to know and understand God better and reach out with His love. I may not know everything about every religion or be an expert on every psycho-sexual issue but I can still operate with the sensitivity, love and acceptance that God directs towards me.

One day I ventured into one of the fast food cafes in the King's Cross area. It turned out to be a meeting place for street people, druggies, pimps, prostitutes, pickpockets, muggers, runaways, etc. I felt like a school kid on his first day at school. I'd no idea what on earth was going on around me! Addicts were falling asleep whilst eating their baked beans on toast. I hadn't the foggiest notion that the girls with whom I was talking were all 'on the game'. (I wondered why they were all so friendly!) I was spending my lunchtimes there, taking a break from the punishing day of preaching on the underground. I am not too sure what my parents and other gentle Christian folk would have said if they had found me in a cafe full of prostitutes and rent boys.

I told my new 'friends' that I was totally straight, didn't know the first thing about prostitution and stuff but was willing to be educated! I then realised what I had just said but, by then it was too late, I'd said it! The girls thought that really funny and I was amazed how quickly they seemed to accept me. Over the months that followed they began to trust me a little and tell me bits about their past life. Their lives were invariably sad.

Generally speaking, a young boy or girl doesn't wake up one morning and say to their self, "I'd think I'd like to follow a career in prostitution!" Most of the lovable characters that I came to know had a story of abuse. Many came from care backgrounds. Some were runaways having had enough of an unhappy life at home. It is so easy for a young person to hit the streets of London and get into prostitution. Imagine you are homeless, cold and hungry and someone offers you a 'free' bed for the night, for a price! You may end up taking drugs or drink just to block out your feelings of guilt. The terrible sense of loneliness and isolation can be very intense. If your only 'friends' are users or are 'on the game' it can be so easy to be drawn into their life style in order just to survive.

One girl shocked me when she told me that I had an Alsatian dog named "Sam" and my wife was from abroad somewhere. (My first wife was Swiss). I thought she had psychic powers and was a little alarmed. What else does this girl know about me? Then, when she told me that she was from Camborne, Cornwall it all began to make sense. She went on to recall that, a few years earlier, I had met her in Camborne square. She had told me that she was homeless and I had invited her back home. I had lent her a sleeping bag and she remembered happily sleeping on the floor of my house, alongside my Alsatian dog. As she recalled the incident everything came flooding back. I could be forgiven for not realising who she was. The girl looked very different now, harder, more street wise and much older.(The harshness of life on the streets of London does not tend to keep you looking young.) She was pleased to tell me that, although she'd been 'on the game' she'd managed to find a hostel and now had a straight job.

There was the time when one of the girls got a beating from her pimp, who was an enormous Caribbean guy. This upset me but I wasn't big enough physically to pull the guy away from the girl. However, I placed myself and my Bible between the pimp and the girl and started preaching to him with all my heart telling him over and over again that "Jesus loved him." This caused a momentary distraction, just long enough to enable the girl to slip away.

Fortunately, the Afro-Caribbean guys have a degree of respect for the preacher and I was never touched. In fact one of the biggest guys that I got to know actually enjoyed me talking to him and insisted that I meet his mum. He was over six foot tall and almost as wide. He had that very placid nature that very large guys sometimes have. After all they don't have to act tough to convince people not to mess with them.

I did go with him to see his mum. She worked in a day nursery nearby. When I saw her I couldn't believe that my big friend could have come out of such a small woman. She was very Caribbean, very small but very loud. Her son introduced me to her as 'his friend the preacher'.

"You don't look like no preacher to me!" she growled.

"I am, honest" I squeaked. "I really love Jesus, I've been telling your boy about him!" I added for good measure.

"You've been telling my boy about Jesus?" she said, grabbing her handbag. "You've been telling my boy about Jesus?" she was shouting now. Without any warning her handbag came thudding down on her son's head. "Well I've been telling my boy about Jesus all through his life" she shrieked "and he still wants to hang round with all dem drug takers….. they just ain't no good for you boy." She then turned on her heels and started on me. "You tell him….you tell him Mr Preacher that they ain't no good for him, he don't listen to me!"

Fortunately I escaped the handbag treatment but I promised I would keep talking to her son about Jesus. He turned up on my doorstep weeks later and was so pleased to have a meal with us, smiling intently at my young kids who were very used to dad turning up with odd characters at mealtimes. In fact my oldest boy, Seth, often developed an instant rapport with our guests. At the age of nine he would begin asking them the most personal of questions "Have you been in prison?" he'd ask. "Do you take drugs?"

Caring for hurting people

My Alsatian dog acted as security for the house and I always felt my family were safe, although looking back on those days we took great risks in running such an 'open home'. One night the police arrived, hunting for a runaway. My wife had informed the children's home about her whereabouts. On discovering that we had 'dobbed her in' to the authorities, the girl had run from our home. By the time the police had arrived she had well gone. Technically, we had done little wrong, having given her a place of safety for the night. We had done the right thing and telephoned the appropriate authorities but the police didn't see it that way. It didn't help that we had another girl answering the girl's description living with us. She had a shaved head as well and when the police put two and two together and made five, the fireworks began! There was much cursing from 'Miss Lookalike' and the situation quickly became a bit tense. Fortunately I was able to convince the officer that she really wasn't the girl in question. Thankfully he believed us and didn't search the property. In the front room we happened to have had another girl staying over night who was a drug user. She admitted the next morning that she was in possession of Heroin and if she had been searched, we also could have found ourselves in trouble if this had been discovered.

On another occasion we had a boy staying in our home for a week detoxing off drugs. I remember praying a lot for him by his bed side. I got the idea to do that from watching 'The Cross and the Switchblade'. He did a lot of sleeping. However, despite all my efforts to tell him about the new life in Jesus, he just disappeared one morning and that was that. I met him months later at the bottom of a tube escalator begging. He was making £80 a day asking for spare change. He was back using drugs again but was so grateful for us putting him up. "It gave my body a chance to recover a little!"

People who live on the streets survive by conning or 'scamming'. There can be little respect for the person who is trying to help them and they may run off with your money or a precious article that they can sell, perhaps to help pay for their habit. They may even 'try it on' with your children, your wife or your husband. I know of Christian families who have been hurt badly from this and are still suffering the consequences. How would you feel if the very person you were trying to help ended up abusing your children, or running off with your husband or wife? Believe me these things happen!

I didn't realise this at the time but I would now argue that our responsibility has firstly to be towards our family. If we are in a street ministry, our home may need to be a 'haven'. It's often draining enough ministering on the streets during the day, without having some damaged person with you in your home, giving off 'heavy duty' vibes all evening. Many are only happy if they are the centre of attention and will manipulate things to the point of soaking up all your time counselling them, or praying with them. Your loved ones don't get a look in and can get very resentful. You might feel you are winning a soul but end up losing your family.

If there is a Christian family in the locality who can take in hurting or homeless people for a period they will be a precious resource to you as a street evangelist. However, this only seems to work when a family is very secure and stable. Personality is also a key element. Nervy, sensitive types don't cope so well as stolid, accepting folk who don't mind calling 'a spade a spade'. These are the types who don't mind laying down and enforcing basic ground rules if they have to. I have met some wonderful down-to-earth, motherly characters who just seem to be able to take on 'all-comers' with the minimum of fuss.

The problem comes when the caring family cannot cope any longer but feel it is their Christian duty to keep going. Often the person they are trying to help can be very insecure and can read rejection into everything. "If you were a real Christian you wouldn't throw me back on the streets." Damaged people can test your love by unsocial behaviour. Once you can't cope with their behaviour, they say, "See, I knew that you were just like the rest!" This type of emotional manipulation can hold you over a barrel.

One way the church could be of help here is to provide an accountability support group for the family who may be willing to take in someone off the streets. The guy or girl needing a home would then have to understand that the support group, not the family has the right to ask them to leave if things aren't working out. In that way, the support group, not the family, would be seen as the 'bad guy' should the arrangement be putting a destructive strain on the family.

Remember, if the homeless person has survived for months on the streets without your help, they can survive again should it prove difficult for them to keep staying with a family. If you are a street evangelist then keep in touch with the person once they leave the Christian family. The individual might feel angry and rejected. Just because the accommodation arrangement failed, doesn't mean that you cease to be their friend.

Another solution is for the church to run a halfway house for street people who want to come off the streets. Youth with A Mission ran such a home in London and I remember they 'babysat' one Irish addict that I knew until he could be admitted to a Christian drug rehab. Remember that few rehabs take people direct from the street. Rather than taking addicts into your home, it might be worth getting to know if there are any organisations in your area who could offer such a safe house resource.

Don't be 'too spiritual' to involve secular agencies that specialise in helping people who are homeless. They often do a great work and we can learn a lot from their experience. Some of these agencies may be suspicious of your Christian motives but can end up having great respect for you if you show humility and reliability. The street pastor scheme has gained respect from local authorities, police and other agencies through their consistent pastoral care on the streets.

Love that goes the extra mile is the only love that is taken seriously amongst street people. My friend gave his shoes away to a guy with no shoes on a cold day. Another friend gave his pullover to a beggar. This is impressive stuff! However you have to be aware of the possibility of manipulation here, for instance, sometimes a beggar would demand that because I was a Christian I should give away my coat to him. "I give things away when God tells me to." I tell such characters. The important thing is that you do not find yourself totally worn out by the manipulation and scams of people, who want nothing to do with Jesus but just want to use you to facilitate their lifestyle.

One addict can sometimes have a loving church running around in circles trying to service their every need. If the addict really wants help to change their life, that's fine but wisdom is needed to make sure that the tail isn't wagging the dog. Our church once called an extra special meeting to discuss the needs of one homeless, alcoholic guy. "Can't you convert some normal guys with not so many problems?" one church leader asked me. The great thing is that when a person from a broken background comes to know Jesus they are often the most effective in bringing others from a similar background to meet Jesus. My wonderful friend, Anita, spent eighteen months living in a Christian home before deciding to come off heroin. She lived in the East End of London and had suffered abuse as a child. After years in the drug scene most of her friends had died and she was heading that way. A Christian friend, Tony Ralls had her stay with his family. She finally met Jesus and years later would accompany me into schools to tell her story to teenagers. Sadly the CRB system can sometimes prevent this from happening today but I recall many staff and children ending up with tears in their eyes as she shared from her heart how Jesus literally saved her.

She would come with me to rock festivals and even came with me to East Germany. One day in Brandenburg, the local youth invited us to their unofficial youth club, held in a dank, old air raid shelter. Bottles were thrown everywhere, neo-Nazi graffiti on the walls, thrash metal playing at full volume. I asked if Anita could tell her story about being rescued from heroin addiction. On hearing the word 'heroin' Anita was given respect and the music was cut. All eyes were on her as she relayed the pain of her years of abuse and addiction. As she started talking about her encounter with Jesus, something supernatural happened; Anita's face began to shine. A literal halo was around her head. The youth who heard her that night became our friends and followed us everywhere, all week, as we preached the gospel in that town.

In King's Cross Anita met a prostitute called Sarah (not her real name). Some Americans had taken Sarah on a Christian camp when she was a little girl. She remembered that when they had prayed for her she had felt this lovely warm feeling, something she had never felt before or after. When Anita introduced me to Sarah I found it very hard to even engage in the conversation with her. She was hard as nails. Years of abuse had knocked any warmth out of her. However, she seemed to trust Anita and we gathered round at the home of another Christian ex-addict. Sarah allowed us to lay hands on her head and pray for her. Suddenly, she fell to the floor like a ton of bricks, almost as if she had been shot. She lay there motionless for quiet a time. When she stood up she was miraculously different. Her eyes were sparkling with love. She had suddenly become all soft and tender. I have never witnessed anything like it. I could now talk with her. She was able to come to church with us and I think even got baptised.

However, despite this supernatural encounter with Jesus, the story does not have a happy ending. I was told that another 'Christian' guy had sex with Sarah and somehow shame seemed to enter into her again. Gone was the joy and softness, she was back to the old, untouchable Sarah.

The last time I saw her, she was soliciting not too far from where I lived in London. I implored her to visit us. Her eyes were dancing all over the place and she begged me to go, pointing out that her pimp was only over in the nearby park. I looked in the direction that she was pointing and sure enough, there was her pimp apparently reading a newspaper. Nothing I could say could change her mind. "I'm lost and that's all there is to it!" she said flatly. She just about let me pray a short prayer for her. I respected her wish that I go before "both of us got hurt". I felt gutted! How could someone meet Jesus so powerfully and then end up back 'on the game'. I comforted myself that Jesus was a friend of prostitutes and notorious sinners and maybe he knew how I felt. It is quite clear that some of his friends also went back to their old life. We can try our hardest, but we can't manipulate people into following Jesus. Sometimes we see glorious acts of the Holy Spirit, only to be frustrated when people walk away.

"Jesus asked 'Didn't I heal ten men? Where are the other nine?" (Luke ch.17 v.17)

In that case 9 out of 10 of those Jesus touched did not come back to seek Him, despite their wonderful healing.

Outside King's Cross Station a group of Christians decided to sing worship choruses. As they sang I sought to share Jesus with onlookers and, every so often would come back to 'warm myself' next to the 'bonfire' of praise and worship. I would get built up by the strong sense of God's presence with the worshippers and then off I would go again.

"What's going on here then?" asked one of the guys from the street.

"These are a bunch of Christians, giving it stick, praising Jesus." I replied.

"Jesus?" he said, his eyes opening wide. "What can Jesus do? I'm a user…can He do anything for me?"

"Well, I could pray for you if you want mate." He seemed to be up for that and I began to pray. I always close my eyes when I pray to shut out distractions. When I opened them the dear boy was nowhere to be seen. "Oh well" I thought "got conned again". Then I looked down and there was the young addict lying flat out on the pavement.

"How did you do that?" the boy said when he opened his eyes.

"I didn't do anything mate, Jesus did!" I stated. I was just as surprised as him.

I wish I could say that this encounter caused the young addict to seek Jesus. To my dismay, while I tried to link him up with a Christian ex addict I caught a glimpse of him embracing a prostitute and walking off with her. I couldn't believe it, the boy had just experienced a powerful encounter with the Holy Spirit and here he was walking away. God does some wonderful things with people on the streets but there are not always squeaky clean endings in the chaotic world of street evangelism.

Will we go where Jesus goes?

I was sitting in one of those super-intense "constipation type" prayer meetings and began shifting from one buttock to another. I love praying but I find these heavy duty, serious affairs aren't my idea of a good time.

"I hope heaven isn't like this" I thought as the spiritual warfare intercessors got going, wrestling with God. I'm all for spiritual warfare and intercession but sometimes people can make it pretty painful stuff. This prayer meeting in a church in Belgium was tough going for me.

I remembered seeing the entrance to a nightclub just next door to the church as I made my way down to the prayer meeting. "What would Arthur do?" I thought. I know the correct thought should have been "What would Jesus do?" but that's not what I thought at the time. I knew exactly what Arthur Blessitt would have done and decided to do the same. Creeping out of the meeting I surfaced near the doorman of the entrance to the club. I grabbed my cross and walked a few yards towards him, holding out my hand and greeting him in English.

Fortunately he spoke a little of my language and was amazed that I was walking from London to Berlin with the cross. In fact, he was so taken by the cross that he called his manager who could speak excellent English. The nightclub manager didn't look the way I thought a nightclub manger should look. He wasn't all steely eyed and hard faced like they appear in the movies. This guy was small and friendly with a kind of nervy personality. We hit it off immediately and laughed a lot. Within minutes I had been invited into the club.

As you know I am the straightest, most 'un-streetwise' guy

around. The worst thing I remember doing as a kid was to be party to the theft of a packet of fruit gums from the local supermarket. Even then, I didn't actually steal them but was merely in on the excitement of the whole escapade. The next worst thing I'd done was smoking in the garden shed as a kid. As an asthmatic that nearly killed me! Finally, the only other heinous thing I remember doing was to be caught snogging my girlfriend in the back of her car by her father. Her father had a temper and my mates called him 'the mad axe man'. Fortunately, he was far angrier with his daughter than he was with me and I escaped the wrath of the axe man. Hardly a colourful past life! I certainly wasn't ready for the sight that greeted me when I entered the bar.

Flesh! Loads of it everywhere! My sheltered upbringing hadn't actually involved me visiting topless bars and here I was trying so hard to be totally nonchalant about the whole thing. I fixed my eyes firmly on my new found manager friend, who was now behind the bar asking me what I would like to drink.

I knew that my role in that club was to stick very close to Jesus and I was soon asking the manger if he had ever given his life to Jesus. Being a Catholic, he knew why Jesus had died but had never accepted forgiveness for his sins or made Jesus his Lord. I asked him if he would like to ask Jesus to take over his life and to my amazement he replied "Yes, why not?" Maybe I should have spent longer explaining it all to him. However, if he was saying yes to Jesus, I wasn't going to hang around for a long discussion. I grabbed his hand and held it while he repeated the 'sinner's prayer'. I sometimes question whether this stuff is real but I will never know if he was really repenting or just going through the motions. He certainly seemed very sincere and thanked me profoundly.

"Do you mind if I pray for the girls?" I asked.

"Go ahead" the manager waved me in the direction to a bunch of topless girls sitting at a table.

"I'm a priest and I've come to pray for you."

I know this isn't strictly true; I'm not an ordained priest. However, the Bible says we are all part of the royal priesthood and for the purposes of praying for topless waitresses it made a lot of sense to call myself a priest. Within hardly any time, with my eyes tightly closed, I was praying my heart out for the girls.

I can't remember if I led them in a prayer to accept Jesus but I do remember them being so grateful for my prayers. As I taught one of them about the need to read the Bible I wasn't even aware of their state of undress. They were girls, just girls needing God's love. I told them I would try to get them Bibles. Fortunately my old mate, Archie, who had been sent into the club to 'rescue me from the den of sin', managed to produce two small Gideon Bibles. However, the manager confiscated these. I guess Bible-carrying topless waitresses didn't look quite right.

I will never know if any long lasting commitments were made but I know God's love was at work in that bar that night. I think that perhaps Jesus would also have taken some time out from the prayer meeting to pop next door to visit the nightclub people. He would have done this on a regular basis as well!

Sexuality and wisdom

Some may argue that it is totally foolish to enter sinful establishments in order to evangelise. "We are simply putting ourselves at risk of temptation and asking for trouble." I know that there is a strong sexual atmosphere in some of the places that I have visited and I wouldn't advise Christians who have a particular weakness in this area to take up this type of ministry.

Every red blooded man can be tempted sexually. A husband and wife partnership is the ideal but this isn't always possible. Equally a male/female partnership can work well, however, if you work with a woman who is not your wife then that too can get complicated. What may start out as an innocent desire to witness together can lead to sharing emotional intimacy. This can very quickly lead to more serious matters. The devil is out to trip us up, especially if we are invading his territory. Street evangelism can leave a person feeling very vulnerable and if the friend you go witnessing with is of the opposite sex, the temptation can be to seek comfort at the end of the day from that person and not your wife or husband. A Christian hug or prayer together can feel a little too good, especially if your partner is very attractive. Don't give the devil a foothold, stick close to Jesus on every turn. Be accountable to another Christian if possible, sharing with them honestly about your struggles.

'The temptations in your life are no different to what others experience. And God is faithful. He will not allow the temptation to be more than you can stand. When you are tempted he will show you a way out so that you can endure.' (1 Corinthians, ch.1 v.13)

The initial temptation is not necessarily 'sin', dwelling on it and letting the devil fan it into flames is what leads you into great danger.

Similarly you have to have wisdom in who you witness to in a nightclub situation. Some make a blanket rule of only witnessing to someone of the same sex. Remember, in a club it is not just people from the opposite sex that 'hit on you'. In one club a gay guy thought it would be fun to poke his tongue down my ear while I was praying for him. It is never straightforward when you are witnessing in clubs, for example, you might start to talk to a mixed-sex group, only to find that the guys leave and you are left talking to the girls. If you start praying with them there is sometimes the possibility of one of them being attracted to you and so the problem begins. My advice is that you walk very close to the Holy Spirit, back off when you need to, make an excuse to leave, go to the toilet, do anything to keep your innocence.

I used to go onto the dance floor and start just worshipping Jesus. I tend to be very expressive in my worship, my arms up in the air while I stomp my feet. Some Christians think I'm too exuberant in my style of worship. However, I never had any complaints on the dance floor; they were up to the same sort of thing although the focus of their 'worship' was perhaps more of a sexual nature! Worship of Jesus is perhaps the most effective way of combating sexual temptation. However, if you really are having problems vacate the club for a while if you must. There's usually a bunch of smokers having a fag-break out there anyway and it is sometimes easier to talk with them without having to battle against the loud music.

I will sometimes ask a mate to come with me just to be my mate. "I'm not asking you to necessarily say anything, just cover me in prayer" This is a great way of involving less extroverted personalities who may die at the thought of being asked to approach a person. What invariable happens is that they accompany you thinking that nothing is expected of them and end up sharing their conversion story anyway. To have a friend like that is invaluable. Not only do they end up praying for you, they often end up joining in when you offer to pray with a club goer. Furthermore, it is usually your quiet natured prayer-friend who ends up getting the 'word of knowledge'. "How come God spoke to them and not me?" I question. It's probably because I was talking too much, yet they were available to listen to the gentle prompts and insight of the Holy Spirit! Your prayer-partner will also be available to you should the unholy atmosphere of the club start to get to you. They can act both as a "Father Confessor" should you be sexually tempted and also as an encourager should the rejection factor start to weaken your spirit.

I had the delight of working with a female law student from an Asian background. She was married to a pastor friend of mine. I gather that she is now a high-powered barrister but is the humblest of characters. The idea was that we were to deliver presents of toiletries (all nicely wrapped up) to prostitutes in Soho. Off we went up the shabby backstairs of buildings, sometimes passing by very furtive looking guys making their way down. The door was knocked and promptly opened, often by a shy Pilipino girl.

"Hi ... we've come to bring you some presents!" my lawyer friend would say in such a loving, natural manner, "Can we come in?"

I would follow her in meekly. I'd never been into visiting brothels before and I wasn't sure what to expect. It was all very normal in some ways. The girls weren't confident sex pots but just ordinary kids who had often come from a children's home background. They were usually very emotionally flat. Nothing was brightly lit and I always left feeling a little hollow. The bright lights of Soho are not very bright at all in reality. It's all quite sad and dingy! However, what filled me with joy was seeing my friend so full of a gentle love. This was Jesus operating through a bubbly little law student. Innocence just oozed from her as she brought a ray of sunshine into these dismal brothels.

Years later I was invited into a brothel in Belgium. It was marginally more upmarket than Soho but the same sadness was there. The girl who had invited us in was a Christian prostitute from Africa. See what I mean? Street evangelism is never straight forward! Here was this happy African girl saying how pleased she was to meet other Christians and she wanted us to read the Bible and pray with her. I think she would have been even more overjoyed if we had had a time of worship as well. She loved Jesus, she really did and she was at pains to point out that she was only there to make enough money to help her family back home. What was I supposed to do? Was I supposed to give her a lecture? Maybe I should have said "Go and sin no more." I'm afraid I was having such a great time praying with her and enjoying Jesus, I didn't have any desire to say that type of stuff.

All I can say is that, Jesus was in me and had filled me with such joy. It just would have gone directly against the spirit to suddenly launch into lecture mode; it just wasn't how the Spirit was leading me. I am obviously not saying that it's fine for Christians to work in the sex trade but, on this occasion, I just wanted to minister love and joy to that dear girl.

One of the girls that I got to know in the King's Cross days was a Scottish high-class prostitute. She preferred to say that she worked as an escort girl. She earned big money but had to make 'mega-bucks' to feed her habit. One day she asked me to see a religious book that someone had given her. Off I went to her flat. The book was duly presented to me to study (it was some Eastern mystic's writings). She disappeared to her bathroom. All I heard was cursing and swearing coming from the direction of the bathroom. Eventually she reappeared apologising for the bad language "I couldn't get the xxxx needle into my toe."

Thinking back I can't believe that I put myself in that situation. I can see the newspaper's headlines, "Evangelist found in the bedroom of high-class escort girl." However, at the time, it seemed the most natural thing to do. She respected me and had grown to trust me.

I remember a few weeks later trying to share Jesus with an old Scotsman at a bus stop. From behind me I heard a familiar voice, "Leave me dad alone you wee little religious pervert you!" I turned to see the high-class escort girl grinning from ear to ear. She was actually delighted that I had met her dad.

Jesus was a friend to notorious sinners and being a friend means being a friend. We can live a righteous lifestyle, stick close to Jesus, but the press and sometimes the church would prefer to question our motives. The problem is, if you are involved in caring for 'non-squeaky-clean people' you can find yourself in 'non-squeaky-clean situations' and the 'squeaky-clean' church doesn't handle this very well.

Years later, while carrying the cross with two of my good mates through part of Romania we found ourselves witnessing to four prostitutes. The older one spoke good English and acted as a translator. As we witnessed to the girls they eventually wanted to pray to receive Jesus. We all knelt down on the street and prayed. The Holy Spirit fell and all of us were crying. It was a beautiful act of God. The older girl possessed a New Testament so I told her she must become the pastor. "Read about Jesus to the girls and whatever He tells you to do, do it!" I encouraged her. The woman thought it very funny to be called a 'prostitute pastor'.

Later I sought to find an ordained pastor to help the girls but was advised that no pastor or his wife would get involved with such a ministry. It was more than their reputation was worth. I can see it from both sides; pastors and street evangelists have to be wise and holy in these situations but what we have to make sure is that we are not controlled by the same Pharisee spirit that Jesus spoke so vehemently against. While we have to act wisely we still need to show the same compassion that Jesus did. Sometimes Jesus ministered to women, sometimes even to single women, sometimes He was even on His own with them and sometimes these single women didn't have the best of reputations!

God's accommodation

On occasions I have had to sleep in some very basic places when I have been carrying the cross. Other times we have been 'forced' to live in luxury! Once, while carrying the cross from Naples to Rome, my wife and I found that the only place available was an upmarket hotel, the type with flags of all nations outside. We were totally exhausted and storm clouds were gathering. We had walked a good twenty miles that day and we were in the middle of nowhere. The next town was a good six miles ahead. "It's going to cost an arm and a leg to pay for this", I thought "It's getting posh-er by the minute." Sure enough it was central London prices. With prayer and cajoling the Catholic owner agreed to give us a single room at a reduced rate but what a single room it was! There are times when Jesus wants to 'comfort us' with a hot shower and towels and dry, clean linen.

Other times I've slept in bus shelters. Once I slept in a barn with cows emptying themselves out throughout the night only yards from my head. On another occasion a young man offered to put me up but on arriving at his flat, I discovered that I was supposed to sleep with him in his double bed. I'd only just met him and wasn't sure of his motivations or inclinations so I made out that I was more than happy to sleep on the chair. The room was thick with dust and being asthmatic, I enjoyed 'a sleepless night' heaving for breath.

One day in Ireland I had spent hours hobbling with my cross, evangelising bedraggled cows in the pouring rain. The West coast can be a little bereft of people at times and the only folk I had witnessed to was a family in a three wheeler van, the type used by 'the Trotters' in 'Only Fools and Horses'.

"That's the greatest act of faith I have ever witnessed" said the dad, a likeable young man with wild hair going in every direction. His little wife beamed encouragingly at me and the little kids laughed in the back of the van. How I love the Irish!

At the end of the day I enquired about bed and breakfast accommodation in the town. "There's only one in the town, just around the corner." Finding the house, I was warmly welcomed by a roly-poly middle aged lady. "At last I can strip off my wet clothes and have a nice bath", I thought as I entered the hall.

"It's alright to leave my cross against the side of the house?" I enquired, more as an after thought than anything.

"What cross? Where?" I proudly showed her the cross leaning against her side wall.

"You can't stay here! No, sorry, I know it's not very Christian of me but we've got enough crosses here thank you very much, you'll have to go!" She meant it, I was soaking. Waterproofs never keep all the rain out. When you stop walking your sugar levels plummet and I was freezing by then .No use arguing, it was back out into the rain for me.

This was not typical of Ireland in any way, I'd been welcomed in by everyone, total strangers had insisted I stay at their place.

Everywhere I had gone I had been given a bed to sleep in. I had even been given a 'Father Ted' presbytery with a little housekeeper lady saying "You will, you will, you will have a cup of tea now won't you?" The priests were even joking about which nuns they fancied, it was straight out of 'Father Ted', I'm not exaggerating in any way!

In one town a man apologised to me that I wasn't able to stay with his family but that he'd 'sort out' a bed and breakfast for me. In the morning I discovered that he had paid for it as well. In another town an alcoholic insisted (I mean I had no choice in the matter) on sticking the cross through the side window of his car and driving me to find my accommodation. How we didn't decapitate any innocent cyclists I don't know. "You didn't get a lift with him" my host asked with a horrified look on his face "he's the local drunk."

I'd known only wonderful Irish hospitality but on this day I was left trudging into town with little money enough for a hotel. I sat in a cafe considering my options. I didn't have many. It was a lonely position to be in. I didn't fancy the bus shelter. Suddenly, I remembered the family that I had met, with the three wheeler van. I half recalled that they had thrust a piece of paper with their address on it. Yes, there at the bottom of my waterproof jacket pocket was the screwed up, soggy piece of paper. I could just make out the address. The home could apparently be found on the council estate. When I was a social worker I could often find the house I was intending to visit without consulting my diary. It was the one with the knee high grass and old washing machine outside. Well, you've guessed it, on this occasion, the very house was the was the one with the long grass etc..

The door opened and a gorgeous little ragamuffin looked at me. "Mam, mam, it's da'fella with d'little cross with the wheel on the end". I was duly welcomed in, they stripped off my soaking clothes, putting them on the Aga ,"I'm afraid we've no hot water" ,they said apologetically. In fact they didn't have a lot of anything, hardly any furniture, no carpets, no light bulbs, nothing! However, they did have dogs, little ones that had left little presents for me to stand in on my way to the toilet at night. A fire was made for me and I was to sleep on a massive cushion under an old bit of carpet, with the dogs.

As I closed my eyes I was just happy to feel loved by a family who had almost nothing but gave what they had to me. In the morning I prayed for them and off I went but as I walked away I was kicking myself for not asking the dad if he would be happy to give his life to Jesus. I should have turned around and gone back but I didn't. However, months later I got a letter from him. It began "Praise the Lord! Praise the Lord! I've got born again." He'd given his life to Jesus anyway. Although I was thrilled, in later months I got a very urgent telephone call from the same guy. He was in London. Apparently things had gone very wrong for him. Could I help him? I arranged to meet him but he never turned up, I just hope that he and his little family have survived. So many of these stories do not have a nice twee ending!

When the bubble bursts

One Irish friend of mine had gone from drug addiction and the rent boy scene to a Christian drug rehabilitation centre and was now on fire for God. He had substituted his drug addiction to an addiction to witnessing and there was no stopping him. He showed great love for his fellow addicts and beggars that we met on the Underground. He testified to thousands on the tubes. What a transformation! However, the bubble burst and he turned back to the addiction and the stealing that went with it. What hurt me was his apparent rejection of me.

One day I got angry with him and made the mistake of pointing my finger. He flipped and I was kicked to the ground and his wife had to force him off me. That really got to me. I had run out of stamina to keep loving and when he telephoned to apologise, to my shame, I was in no mood to forgive. I should have got back in touch and I didn't. I was worn out and felt 'used'. However, that's no excuse and I should have kept going. How we need God's love when we run dry. I am not sure if he is still alive but if he is I ask for forgiveness for shutting down on him.

God's sat nav

"Where are you wanting to go?" The African lady demanded.

"Holloway" I replied.

It was 2 o'clock in the morning, I had no money for a taxi, I'd already done a day's walk with the cross in France and had taken the train, the ferry, and finally had hitch hiked the last leg of the journey to London. Ending up in Stratford, East London, I was supposed to give a talk on street evangelism later that day at a conference. Friends who lived near Holloway Prison had offered to put me up but that was nine miles away. I thought I would try hitch hiking but only got rude rebuffs from everyone. Then a car stopped with a single black woman at the driving wheel. Single women do not pick up single guys at 2am in London!

As I crawled into the passenger seat I thought I had better give my full credentials just in case the lady was a 'lady of the night'. I wanted to get things straight at the start of the journey.

"I'm a Christian" I informed her.

"Praise Jesus!" she shouted, "Praise Jesus!" "My Jesus told me to pick you up but I said to my Jesus…..he might have a gun!"

"Even if he has a gun you pick him up" my Jesus said. She went on, "I saw them bad, bad people swearing at you when you asked for a lift so I thought my Jesus wants me to give you a lift."

I lay my head on the headrest and tears filled my eyes. What is the chance of anyone, let alone a single Christian lady giving me a lift in East London at 2 o'clock in the morning? To my amazement the dear African lady began speaking in tongues at the top of her voice. This went on for quite a time until she stopped and turned to me.

"Excuse me speaking in tongues darling, but I don't know the way to Holloway so I am asking Jesus the way to get there!"

Well I'm not sure about the 'Jesus sat nav' but we turned left and right, left and right, through Hackney marshes and all sorts of places. However, sure enough there in front of me eventually was 'Holloway Prison'. Throughout the journey I had heard how she had been miraculously cured of HIV. Even part of her uterus had been removed but x-rays had shown that she now had a brand new uterus. She told me that she would leave work at 6pm and go to her church each evening and there she would 'do business with God'. There she would 'pray and pray and pray and pray'; there she would 'stomp on Satan's head!' I believe it! I think I would be terrified of her if I was a demon. She was wonderful! I will probably never see her again until I get to heaven but when I do I'll find her there still stomping on Satan's head.

Jesus goes everywhere, to the streets, the pubs, the clubs, the topless bars, the brothels, the posh places and the poorest places. I have found him in all these places, even in a car driven by a single black lady in the early hours of the morning.

CHAPTER 4

GETTING TO THE POINT

Ten difficult questions
Praying the prayer
So how do I present the gospel?
Is it necessary to ask someone to pray out loud?
Is the person saved once they say the prayer?
Immediate aftercare
What if the person doesn't feel different after
praying the prayer?
Your baby

Ten difficult questions

Why is it that people from rough and ready lorry drivers to young teenagers to cultured businessmen come up with the same arguments against receiving Jesus? The wording and accents may vary but the excuses are the same.

The Bible makes it clear that we are fighting with evil forces that are seeking to blind the person from seeing the truth. We shouldn't be surprised when we see the 'lord of this world' struggling to prevent an individual from being won over to the kingdom of light.

I have noticed here, an interesting phenomenon. There seems to exist a kind of CD containing ten or more tracks that the devil seems to insert into people's minds. For example, I may seek to talk to somebody about Jesus and immediately the devil selects a track. "The Bible contradicts itself!" someone may say, regardless of whether they have read the Bible. If you suggest that you name some of the contradictions they are often not able to point to any. Obviously there are some slight differences in the gospel writers' accounts but you would expect people to have slight differences in the way they recalled an incident. However, in this instance they rarely want to wait for an answer but merely want to voice an objection. Where did they get the objection from? I believe it is simply the devil trying to create barriers against them turning to God. "Who made God?"

someone may say, cackling away. Do they really want an answer? Often they don't.

When this happens I have been known to say to them, "The devil has put that question into your mind!" Interestingly I have never yet had anyone disagree with that statement. It is often possible to waste hours 'sword fencing', debating with people who clearly don't want to know Jesus. If they say "Yes but" to anything you say they really mean "No!" I will often bow out of the conversation at that point. Sometimes a drunk, hoping for a good argument may try to goad me into a debate. "You are too scared to argue with me" he may say trying to appeal to my pride. In that case, it is just best to walk away.

Seek to be respectful to all, but always focus your attention on those who are open, not those who closed. Often the devil places someone in a group to throw in arguments. It may sound rude but I often turn my back on the troublemaker in order to give my undivided attention to the person who is genuinely interested. Often the troublemaker would tire of his sport and leave you in peace. If you let them divert you into answering their questions, they end up controlling the situation.

However, despite all this, there are times when it **is** worth seeking to answer genuine questions. In the Bible we read that Paul debated and sought to pull down arguments against the truth.

"We are human but we don't wage war as humans do. We use

God's mighty weapons, not worldly weapons, to knock down the strongholds of human reasoning and to destroy false arguments. We destroy every proud obstacle that keeps people from knowing God." (2 Corinthians Chapter 10 v3-5)

Paul had a great mind but knew the problem was a spiritual one with human pride at the centre.

Recently a young man wanted to debate Christianity but I asked him if I could pray for him first. I did this and then began to seek to answer his questions. I fought spiritually first, rather than trying to argue him into believing. We have to operate in the spirit in order to sense if a person is receptive to the truth. If they are, it is worth seeking to answer their questions.

We are told to give a 'reason for the truth that is within us'. It is good then, to look at some of the common excuses and possible answers to some of the things that people say. Although there are many more questions, these are some of the more common ones that people put to me.

Ten difficult questions

1

I only believe
what I can see

Possible answers:

You can't see electricity or wind, but you can see its effect! The
Bible teaches that no living person can see God, since God is
too brilliant to be seen. Even part of His creation, the sun, is too
brilliant to look at with a naked eye, so how can you possibly see
God.

However, it is possible to see evidence of God's existence
through:

1. **His creation**. Such an amazing design would require a
   designer.

2. Through **our conscience.** Where does our sense of right and
   wrong come from?

3. Through **Jesus**, He claimed to be God in human form and
   gave convincing proof to support His claim, "Anyone who
   has seen Me has seen the Father." said Jesus. (John Chapter
   14v9b)

4. Through **miracles**. The changed lives, healings, deliverance
   and other answers to prayer that many Christians have
   experienced.

I believe the reason why the devil puts this thought into people's
heads is because he wishes himself to blind people from seeing
the real evidence of God.

I only
believe
what I
can see

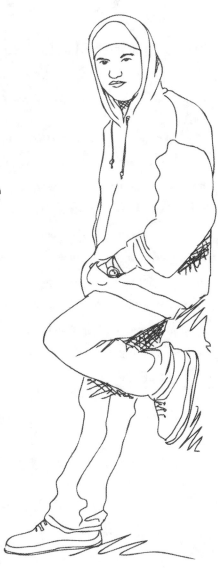

Science disproves God

Possible answers:

Many scientists are convinced Christians. It has been said that "Scientists are simply discovering God's thoughts after Him!" The more scientific knowledge we gain the more we discover that the world has an amazing design. It is logical to presume that such a design would require a designer. The creation versus evolution argument is centred on interpretation of the evidence available. Evolution is a 'theory', not a 'fact'. There are scientists who feel that the evidence available points to the Bible creation account. I believe the reason why the devil puts this obstacle in people's minds is that he would rather people worship 'science' than the God who created it.

Science
disproves
God

It's all in the mind

It's all in the mind

The thinking\behind this argument is that Christian conversion is based on self-fulfilment. It is argued that we change because we, or others around us, want ourselves to change.

Possible answers:

1. "A person can't pick himself up by his own shoelaces." A person who has never received love, finds it difficult to give love and so a never-ending circle of deprivation is started. Christian conversion, breaks into that circle and even many hardened people such as criminals or addicts claim that it is the outside power of God that has transformed them not a power that they found within themselves. A diversity of people are transformed from different backgrounds (ie different countries, cultures, classes, intelligence levels, etc). This makes it difficult to explain it away on the basis of conditioning. Many have been converted without the outside influence of friends, of family, of church or even a Bible.

2. Conversion is not just based on people's 'experience', but on the person of Jesus Christ who promised to change people's lives. The evidence shows that not only did He exist but that He also claimed to be the Son of God; was crucified and came back to life again. You must judge the <u>facts</u> of Jesus as well as the evidence of those who claim to have been changed by Him. I believe the devil hates Christian conversion and influences people to try and explain it away.

4

Christians are hypocrites

Possible answers:

1. A 'hypocrite' is someone who says that he is good but acts otherwise. However, a Christian is someone that admits that he is bad and is in need of Jesus. Indeed he calls on Jesus for the power to change.

2. Jesus was not a hypocrite. He lived consistently to his own teaching. He hated hypocrisy! He challenged His close friends to point out any hypocrisy in Him but they were unable to do so. Even if some Christians are guilty of hypocrisy Jesus was not! First, look at Jesus who was perfect, before looking at His followers who are imperfect.

I believe the devil hates the church, which is God's 'bride', and so influences everyone to be critical of it.

Christians are hypocrites

5

Religion is the main cause of wars

The argument here is that, religion has often been a major contributory factor in so many of the conflicts that have occurred down through the ages. (It is said that, at any one time in history, there has usually been around 40 wars being fought.) By implication therefore, religion cannot be a good thing! Some would go as far as to blame God for war itself!

Possible answers:

1. It is true that throughout history many have used their religion to commit violence. If you study the facts you will often discover that it was their religious, political or personal views that they have followed and certainly not the teachings of Jesus.

2. Jesus was known as the Prince of Peace and taught people to love their enemies. The true follower of Jesus finds himself seeking reconciliation with those that he may have hurt or with those who have done him wrong.

I believe the devil is 'the lord of this world' and he is the 'god of destruction'. He is the spiritual influence behind war.

Religion is the main cause of wars

6

The Bible is exaggerated

The Bible is exaggerated!

This argument is usually based on the thinking that, in the person's experience, the supernatural does not occur. Therefore, the miracles that occurred in the Bible or Jesus' claim to be the Son of God, must be 'Chinese whisper' exaggerations. It is therefore argued, that Jesus was a wise man but down through the ages the story has been blown out of all proportion.

Possible answers:

1. Non-Christian historical evidence confirms that Jesus existed and that he claimed to be the Son of God and that He was crucified and that His followers claimed that He had come back to life again three days later.

2. Archaeological discovery supports rather than disproves the Bible! The book of Luke for example, is seen by historians as exceptionally accurate.

3. The New Testament writings, Matthew, Mark, Luke and John, have far greater historical evidence than any other of the historical events and characters that existed at that time (the authenticity of which are usually accepted without question.)

4. Why should many of the Bible writers be prepared to die for what they know to be a pack of lies?

I believe the devil hates the Bible because it is the Word of God. He has always sought to influence people to question its accuracy or credibility.

I've nothing against the teachings of Jesus it's just that I don't need Him myself

7

The thinking behind this statement is that, while the moral teaching of Jesus, such as" love your neighbours" is seen to be good, it is felt that his teaching can be followed without having to have a personal relationship with Jesus.

Possible answers:

1. Apart from the moral teaching of Jesus He also taught that He was the Son of God. If this was not true, then He would have to either be mad, or a liar, neither or which are a good qualification to be a great moral teacher. Many would argue that you can't pick some of Jesus' teachings and leave the rest.

2. Jesus also taught that it is impossible for man to get into heaven through human means. Following His moral teaching is not enough! He taught that His death was to buy forgiveness of sins. Only acceptance of this has opened the doorway to heaven.

I believe the devil is happy for people to pride themselves into thinking that they are too good to need to accept Jesus' death for them. They think that they can be good without Jesus. Jesus did not teach this!

I've nothing against the teachings of Jesus, it's just I don't need him myself

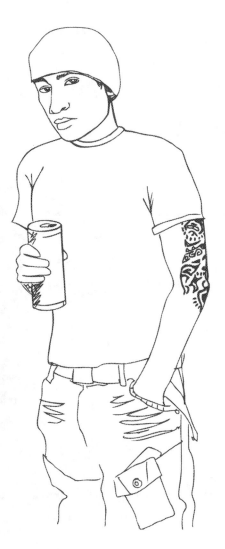

8

What about other religions?

The thinking behind this question is that it is arrogant and unloving to say that we can only reach God through Jesus.

Possible answers:

1. Other great religious leaders only claim to point the way to God, not to be God themselves. Only Jesus claimed to be God and provided the evidence in terms of His teachings, His perfect life, His miracles and His resurrection as proof to support His claim.

2. Jesus said that He is "the truth". If this is correct, He must be the plumb line to determine what is true and false in other religions. All other religions depend on some form of ladder of self-effort (good works, religious observance or mystical experiences) by which it is hoped that a person can reach God or gain eternal happiness. They do not offer the assurance of forgiveness of sins or eternal life. It is only Jesus who does that!

I believe the devil would love to relegate Jesus into being seen as just another great religious leader and not part of the Godhead.

What about other religions?

9

What about suffering?

What about suffering?

The thinking behind this question is that, a God of love wouldn't allow suffering. It is argued that, suffering shows that God does not exist or, that if He does exist, He is either unloving or unable to relieve suffering.

Possible answers

1. Much of the world's suffering is caused by the selfishness of man, i.e. broken homes, wars, car accidents, lack of money or the will-power to tackle starvation or disease. The Bible teaches that natural disasters, illness, death, etc. started only when man disobeyed God. Both man and nature itself, was corrupted by this act. Jesus also promised that in this world we will have trials and tribulations. (John Chapter 16 v 33b)

2. God has not made Himself immune to suffering. However, although on many occasions, Jesus sought to eliminate suffering in man, he did suffer Himself. He was well acquainted with painful human emotions. He suffered an incredibly horrific death in order to demonstrate God's love.

3. The Bible also teaches that suffering in this life is only

comparatively short compared with an eternity in heaven where there is no suffering. Christians who have suffered have often claimed that God has comforted and strengthened them through their suffering. Certainly many who have suffered have reflected God's character even more than those who haven't suffered.

4. Many have claimed healing through God-given medical treatment or through God actually touching them directly.

5. Ultimately, there is no complete answer to this question! Some people haven't been healed even after faithful prayer.

I believe the problem of suffering is one of the devil's favourite obstacles to place in people's minds. I believe he is seeking to pin the blame on God for something for which the devil is actually responsible.

10

We are all God

The thinking behind this statement is that, God is everywhere and therefore, He is in everything, including ourselves. It is argued that, we human beings, have no need to repent of our sins or to invite Jesus to become the Lord of our life but we simply have to *'realise the God that is within us'*.

Possible answers:

1. While the Bible says that God is everywhere, has created everything and has made man with qualities of love, justice, etc. it also points out that man has never been God. When man disobeyed God he was spiritually separated from Him.

2. Jesus is the only person who has offered convincing evidence that He is God in human form. The person who says he is god brings God down to his own level. Such a person denies the teaching of Jesus concerning man's sin and God's holiness and has no use of Jesus' death for his sins.

I believe the devil was thrown out of heaven for wanting to be worshipped as God. He has not stopped trying to influence people to think that they also are able to be 'as God'.

We're all God

The author is grateful to 'Agape' for use of some of their material included in 'Ten Difficult Questions'

Praying the prayer

"Ok, why are you carrying the cross?" the bright young Italian girl asked confidently. In fact she was so sure of herself I felt sure she must be a reporter. She had emerged from the Rome film studios, Italy's version of Hollywood. I continued to answer her many questions. "Which countries have you carried the cross through? Why do you do it?"

A short time into the interview her whole approach changed. She suddenly began telling me about her personal life, recounting how her father had died a few years ago and how the bottom of her world had fallen away. She had become totally bereft and had begun searching for something to fill the ache that she felt in her heart. She tried boyfriends, going from boy to boy but still there was that emptiness inside. She tried drinking and drugs to mask the pain. She even tried to go to a local Catholic church to find God but where was God? She couldn't find Him!

At this point she began to cry. I'm not too good with women crying and thought it best if my wife took over. Deb arrived and she immediately embraced her. Now both of them were sobbing. "Weep with those who weep!" After a few minutes my wife simply asked, "You'd life to receive Jesus wouldn't you?"

"Yeah, yeah, I wanna know Jesus" she spluttered.

"Why don't you pray this with me?" Deb said softly. "Jesus, thank you for loving me."

The girl began to copy each sentence:

"Thank you for dying for me."

"Jesus, please wash away my sins."

"Jesus, come into my heart, I give my life to you."

By now I was also crying! Here was a spiritual baby being born on the streets. For the last forty years I have lived to see this sort of thing happen, something broke in me and I wept from a place deep inside of my heart. This was real.

As the girl dried her eyes she began squinting at the sky. "I feela different!" she exclaimed in her delightful Italian accent, "Why do I feela different? Look, the sky is blue, everything looks so different."

I remember a former witch telling me that before she met Jesus everything seemed to be like a black and white television. However, after Jesus had come into her life it was more like watching a colour television. Suddenly the beauty of God's creation had been revealed to her. Now here was this Italian girl experiencing the same thing. We had not spent hours explaining the gospel; she had not been attending an Alpha course. (That is a "just looking" type course for those interested in understanding the Christian faith or for those actually searching for God). We had not answered a lot of complicated questions about God. We had simply led her in a prayer. However, God clearly met her at her point of need.

Jesus typically did exactly that while he was in bodily form.

He met people at their point of need. This is the starting point for most of us when we become Christians. It may be that a Christian had helped us with a practical problem and this has sparked a desire for us to find Jesus. Maybe a Christian has prayed for our healing and this very act of love had made us interested in finding Jesus. If we are miraculously healed the doors of our heart are often open to inviting Him in to take over our life! Maybe it is prayers for deliverance, as it was for the witch mentioned a little earlier. She was delivered from her darkness and now wanted the light. This is the point that John Wimber makes in his book 'Power Evangelism'. A power encounter with Jesus can often (but not always) result in commitment to Jesus.

The heart of the gospel is that Jesus wants to meet our needs, our needs for love, joy, peace, forgiveness, for salvation. I was fortunate to listen to the great evangelist, Billy Graham preach. I expected something akin to show business. It wasn't! It was a humble man seeking to show us our need of Jesus. After listening to him preach I remember thinking "I could have said that! He made it so simple!" Yet the crowds would come surging forward to respond to Billy's challenge. The truth is, the gospel <u>is</u> simple. God wants it that way. Our role in the street is to get people to realise that they have a need for Jesus. They are out there!

"For the Son of Man has come to seek and to save those who are lost." said Jesus   (Luke Chapter 19 v10).

The reason we go on the streets is because that is where people are. They are in the pubs and clubs because they are looking for something. Almost everyone I meet agrees that they are looking for love. Most agree that they get drunk to get happy, they are searching for joy. A great surge in smoking cannabis only shows that people don't have peace but are simply searching for an artificial 'peace' through a chemical. Many get involved in the occult practises or Eastern religions because they are searching spiritually. Magazines are often full of advertisements for psychics seeking to sell their wares. There is a vacuum and, if it is not filled with the living God, people will seek to fill it with artificial gods.

So how do I present the gospel?

The salesman is taught that his initial task is to help his customer see that he has a 'need' for the product. Then he must go on to show how his product can meet this perceived need. It is not being unspiritual to say that there are parallels with the gospel. We must help people see their need for Jesus and then show how Jesus can meet their need.

Some people tell me that I am too quick to get people to pray 'the sinner's prayer'. They tell me that repentance is the first step to Jesus. A favourite method used by some evangelists is to go through the 10 Commandments and then show how each one of us has probably broken all of them at one time of another.

For example, the point is made that if we have ever lied, then that makes a liar. If we have ever looked lustfully at a married woman, then since Jesus taught that in God's sight, thoughts are the same as intentions, then this would make us an adulterer and so on. This is, of course a very effective way of helping people see the extent of their personal sin.

I would agree that a sense of sin and a desire for repentance (doing a U-turn towards God) is essential for a person to get his life right with God but I have come to see that spirit of true repentance has to exist within the individual himself! It is not up to me to rub their nose in their sin so they feel guilty enough to need Jesus. It is the Holy Spirit that creates a conviction of sin.

"And when He (the Holy Spirit) comes He will convict the world of its sin." (John Chapter 16 v 8a)

The idea of the preacher telling the whole world that they are all going to hell rarely seems to have the desired effect. However, there are times when a simple explanation of the gospel can have the effect of helping people to see their need to turn to God.

"For I am not ashamed of the good news about Christ, for it is the power of God at work, saving everyone who believes." (Romans Chapter 1 v16a).

There is a power in the gospel message that helps people to see their need but also to see how Jesus is the only one who can meet their need.

Some may say that all we need to do is to tell our story of how Jesus touched us and then ask people if they want Jesus. The problem is that our 'testimony' of meeting Jesus may not involve a full explanation of the gospel. To say "I was brought up in a Christian home and heard about Jesus and then went to a Christian festival and felt the presence of Jesus" is not the full story. "Each to his own, I'm pleased to hear you've found what's good for you" says the nice friendly guy. "I have no need for such an experience."

A surfer might say "I often feel one with nature while surfing." The drug taker might talk of 'spiritual' experiences.
"I met God" said one young girl to me.
"Great, what happened?" I replied.
"I met God on the moon and she's not male, she's female!" she replied earnestly. It turned out that she was into the occult in a big way. She certainly believed that she had a testimony of meeting God but was it the real God?

Our 'experience' then, is not necessarily the full gospel. People from cults and other religions can speak of experience. Some tell me that "everyone's experience is valid; no one can say that they have a monopoly on truth". If you speak about a life change they reply that a self-improvement course can do the same thing. Maybe you could try to convince them by using a story of healing. "It's amazing the power of mind over matter" they reply. Our testimony of meeting Jesus should go hand in hand with the message of the gospel. However, when I have asked mature Christians, who have followed Jesus for years, to explain the gospel they have often made it very complicated. The gospel is in fact very simple. I believe it can be boiled down to four statements:

1. The love of God
2. The problem of man.
3. God's solution.
4. Our response

The Love of God

My starting point is that I always believe that God loves the person that I'm talking to. He understands them and wants to have a relationship with them. Many people feel lonely and misunderstood but have to hide behind a mask of 'being sorted'. To hear that there is a God who is interested in them can be good news.

I use the Bible to back up the statement. The dynamics change when you open the Bible. People either get scared or feel challenged. There is an authority in the Bible.

"The Word of God is alive and active." (Hebrews Chapter 4 v12)

I remember meeting a young guy in New Zealand who had just come out of prison. He had met born again Christians in prison and his girlfriend had just started going to church. When we talked about being born again he hovered around the subject, not wishing to commit himself. However, when I opened the Bible his eyes were transfixed by the words and he was soon praying to accept Jesus. No sooner had we all finished praying together, when two large motorbikes roared up. Off got an enormous Maori guy with a face covered with tattoos. It transpired that he was a born again ex-leader of a notorious Maori gang. He and his mate had spotted the cross and the open Bible.

"Let's have a prayer meeting." I said and soon the new Christian was feeling the love of the Holy Spirit and the warmth of his new-found brothers.

The Bible is powerful and it doesn't matter if we look like a Jehovah Witness. "I am a Bible basher." I say joking while I open my Bible. I tell people "This Bible is brilliant; the words in this book will blow your head off." I day-glow the 'juicy verses' and show them to people. I present for instance; John Chapter 3 v 16 or 1 John Chapter 4 v9 and then ask them, "What do you think this means?" If you get the person to read the verse, you are often halfway there. Often the Holy Spirit does the rest. They end up telling you what the verse is saying.

The Problem of Man

"For everyone has sinned; we all fall short of God's glorious standard." (Romans Chapter 3 v23).

It is important to help people understand that our sin causes a problem between God and ourselves. When I use the word 'sin', I usually refer to it as the problem of human nature. People from countries such as Romania, Sri Lanka and Bangladesh are often quick to agree that corruption and greed can be a major problem in their country. To make it more personal, I will often admit my own sins of selfishness, gossip, pride, etc to people. I point out that even the nicest people I meet around the world struggle with the same human nature as I do. I refer to the problem of sin as the 'cancer' of human nature. It is this cancer that has created the barrier between us and God.

I use illustrations all the time. In fact Jesus didn't teach anything without using a parable to back it up.

"Jesus always used stories and illustrations like these when speaking to the crowds. In fact He never spoke to them without using parables" (Matthew Chapter 13 v34)

I might for example, grab a coke tin and pretend to put cigarette ash in it to pollute it. "You wouldn't drink something that's not pure would you?" I ask. "If we who are dirty got into heaven, we'd pollute heaven and it would no longer be pure! Jesus needs to purify us before we can get into heaven."

There are so many illustrations we can use. Just ask the Holy Spirit and you will be surprised how He will inspire you with ways to illustrate the point you wish to make.

When I used to preach on the tube trains, I felt sure that the advertising companies were operated by Christians. They would design advertising wall posters that would be perfect for a gospel preach. "Over here ladies and gentleman there is a poster saying three steps to heaven". (It might have been advertising perfume but I wasn't bothered.)

Any person with a truthful heart will admit that they struggle with sin. One illustration that I have sometimes used is the following. Suppose in one day, we do three things that offend God. We say one wrong thing, we think one wrong thing and we do one wrong thing. That would mean that in a year we will have done 1,000 wrong things. Now if you multiply that by our age, then we can see the problem. A twenty five year old would face God with 25,000 sins.

As mentioned previously, I never feel that it is my job to make people hate their sin. This is the work of the Holy Spirit. Many people tell me that they don't like themselves at times and feel a 'yucky' feeling when they do wrong. At this point they are starting to realise that they have a guilt problem. What's the solution?

God's Solution

It is one thing to agree that we are sinners but another thing to be truly sorry and have a longing to be different. The illustration is given that, if the pass mark for an exam is 50% then those with 49% fail, along with those who score only 5%. The problem for those people who score 49% is that they often feel that they deserve to get to heaven because they aware of their own goodness. Those who score 5% usually have a greater sense of their own sin. They have failed and they know it. The addict, the alcoholic, the prisoner and the adulterer often feel that there is no hope 'for the likes of them' of getting into heaven.

Before carrying the cross from Naples to Rome, my wife and I had the privilege of being prayed for by a collection of recovering addicts. They laid hands on us and prayed with such a love and compassion. When they began worshipping the Lord you could see how much they truly loved God. "How come these guys love God so much?" I asked the church leader. "He who is forgiven much, loves much!" came the reply. "Some of these guys have lived through hell before they met God." "God lives in that high and lofty place with those whose spirits are contrite and humble." (Isaiah Chapter 57 v15)

It is the person who is aware of his own failings who is truly

grateful and responsive to God's own solution. For those
who can grasp firmly the truth found in Romans Chapter 3 v23
and who know that they fall short of God's standard, then the
following verses may well appear to be amazing news.
"For the wages of sin is death but the free gift of
God is eternal life through Christ Jesus our Lord"
(Romans Chapter 6 v 23)
"But God showed His great love for us by sending
Christ to die for us while we were still sinners."
(Romans Chapter 5 v 8)
There are many illustrations to demonstrate what God has done
to provide a solution. There is, for example, the story of the
judge who finds that his own son stands before him guilty of an
offence. Justice is required that the boy is fined heavily for the
offence. However, the judge knows that his son cannot pay the
fine and comes down from his judge's seat and pays the fine for
his son, so that the boy can go free.
Another favourite of mine, is the story of the brothers. The
younger brother murders someone and goes to his older brother
for help. The older one takes the murder weapon from him,
together with his younger brother's jacket stained with blood.
"If the police arrest me and I am executed for this murder" says
the older brother, "you must promise me that you will start living
a good life." The police arrested the older brother and he was
indeed wrongly executed. When the younger brother heard

of his brother's death, it broke him and from that moment he started to live a good life.

Many have seen the film, 'The Passion of Christ' and are aware of how much Jesus suffered on the cross. When I was a boy, a preacher gave me a blow by blow account of what it must have felt like to be crucified. He finished his talk by saying "Next time you see a picture of Jesus dying for you remember that you caused Him to be killed." I was perturbed and upset to hear this. I had always hero worshipped Jesus and felt that I would never have wanted Him killed. I expressed how I felt to my dad and will always remember his reply. "Lindsay, Jesus died for the human race, are you part of the human race?" The penny had dropped! I knew the failings in my human nature and, at that moment I realised, that Jesus had died for me.

In Bangladesh many people do not know the meaning behind the cross. When I have explained it to them it is wonderful to see them understand, for the first time in their life, that Jesus is the Lamb of God who takes away the sin of the world. Indeed, that he can take away their personal sin.

Sometimes large crowds have gathered and I have had to preach my heart out. Faced with such great gatherings I would often feel a great sense of inadequacy. "Where is Reinhart Bonke when you need him?" (Reinhart is a German Evangelist who has preached to massive crowds, especially in Africa) However, it has been an absolute joy to preach the message of the cross! Indeed, I believe it creates great joy in heaven when the message is preached! Furthermore, I have witnessed the joy on earth of seeing people for the first time realise that Jesus has personally died for them, it is all very thrilling.

Once I heard an incredible story concerning the operator of a swing bridge. The bridge took a railway line over a river. One day the operator's young son had clambered down and had begun playing amongst the cogs that worked the swing bridge. The operator had no idea that his son was there. When it came the time to close the bridge in order to allow the fast approaching passenger train to cross, he looked down and to his horror, he saw his son playing in the machinery below. What was he to do? If he left the swing bridge open and went to rescue his son, then the train would plunge into the river, hundreds would be killed. If he closed the bridge then hundreds would be saved but his own son would be killed.

What did he do? Fighting back the tears he closed the bridge knowing that his son would be horribly crushed. He looked down at the passengers as the train passed by. They were totally oblivious to the immense sacrifice that had just been made. They were sleeping, eating ice creams, looking out the window, reading books, they had no idea.

I told that story to a collection of heavily tattooed muscle men in Sheffield. They were laughing at my antics of carrying the cross. Many of them were Catholic lads and had crosses tattooed on their back. When I told the story of the swing bridge operator there was total silence. No more jokes. I knelt and led them in a prayer of thanks to God for His sacrifice for us. In England, I have found that it isn't so much that people haven't heard of Jesus' death, it's just that they haven't realised the depth of how much has been sacrificed to buy the possibility of forgiveness. In Asia, I will often use the 'Bridge to Life' way of explaining the gospel because it is so visual. I draw in the dust two cliffs facing each other. The gulf between them is caused by God being holy and man being sinful.

I will then show man's attempt through religion to get back to God. Many Muslims understand this and know that it is impossible to become a perfect Muslim.

I then show God's solution of sending a human version of Himself to the world to show us what God is really like. I have seen both Hindu's and Muslims start to grasp this point.

Finally, I explain how Jesus' death created a bridge for sinful men to cross over to God.

In Nepal I used a filthy sewer to illustrate the gulf created by our sin. I used a person to illustrate 'God' standing one side of the sewer. I then explained that I represented a human being standing on the other side, unable to cross the 'sin gap'. The crowd loved it!   My builder friend, 'Big Dave', acted as Jesus and with his spade-sized hands, effortlessly lifted me over the sewer to 'God'. The crowd clapped and understood that Jesus wanted to do that for us. At that point, a woman spoke up saying that, six months ago; she also" let Jesus carry her over the sewer". She then went on to relate her own conversion story.

Man's Response

Our calling is not to shove religion down people's throats. It is in fact, impossible to force anyone across the 'bridge to God'. I remember imploring a young addict in Sheffield to accept Jesus. He understood the good news but was not ready to receive it for himself. I was so frustrated that he wouldn't receive Jesus. It is very hard to pull apples off trees when they are not ready. God may have sent the rescue helicopter above the drowning drug addict. The death of His Son Jesus may have provided the rope. We may be shouting from the helicopter "Grab the rope" but if the person won't grab it, we have to accept that God has done all that He can to try to rescue that person. The person has to allow himself to be rescued.

Another illustration I love using is that of the Glastonbury rock festival ticket. The tickets are now very expensive and often hard to get. I ask young people to imagine that their dad has sacrificed greatly and managed to buy a ticket as a gift. If you paid him for it then it wouldn't be a gift. Imagine that you know about the ticket, but when the actual Glastonbury weekend comes, you don't bother to go. Your dad would be jumping! He'd be well upset about it! What an absolute waste!

Our Father in heaven has provided a free gift to a rock festival that goes on for all eternity but we have to receive that gift in order to gain entry. Jesus has bought us forgiveness of sin but if we refuse this forgiveness then, no matter how great the cost, this gift will be wasted on us and we will be unable to get into heaven.

However, thank God, there are many people who **are** ready to receive the gift. Others may have sought to share Jesus with them in the past and their heart is prepared.

Let me share some stores from New Zealand. In twenty days my friend, Dave, and I walked from Auckland to Wellington carrying the cross. We averaged some twenty miles a day. Ridiculous mileage! It was very tough going! "Where were all the people?" we thought, as we slogged along mile upon mile of open countryside. We wondered if God wanted us to preach to the sheep instead! Yet, despite this, God did have 'human sheep' that He had arranged for us to meet.

At one point on the walk, we stayed with a real live 'Crocodile Dundee' character. He lived up in the middle of the New Zealand hill country, a hunter by trade, his house was filled with all sorts of trophies and magazines about shooting and fishing etc. He delighted in sharing with us, his love of life in the wild.

"Gonna be a bit rough today, lads" he grunted, as we left. He was right, the rain started and in a few hours we became totally miserable. Rain always gets in down your neck; your feet get wet and blister up quickly. It is no picnic at times.

"Let's get out the rain" I shouted to Dave, "here's a cafe."
The little cafe was deserted but eventually the owner turned
up, a likeable old guy of retirement age. He thought we were
cyclists at first but when we showed him the cross he became
intrigued and insisted on us "meeting the wife". As we entered
their house, Dave and I felt strangely 'at home'. Dave, in fact,
started taking off his wet clothes and hanging them over the
stove.

Even before we had properly introduced ourselves the wife
started up with, "We feel that something's missing in our lives."
The Holy Spirit within me was stirring in excitement and unable
to contain myself, I asked if we could pray with her.

As soon as I had finished praying she told me that, "she'd got
this letter". She thrust a handwritten letter under my nose.

It was a letter from her brother who was a missionary in the
Philippines. The letter started something like this; "You know
that you were saying that there was something missing in your
life, well I believe that, what is missing, is Jesus." Her brother
had then gone on to explain the gospel in the letter, together
with a prayer of commitment written out at the end.

"Have you prayed this prayer?" I asked. "Well, no" they said
hesitantly.

"Would you like to pray this prayer?" I pushed gently.

"Well, err... err,..... well yes ..!" they said sincerely.

What a moment! I could hardly believe it was happening! I hadn't even taken a sip of my coffee. We could feel the presence of Jesus in the house as they prayed the prayer to receive Him into their lives. As they finished praying the words came into my mind; "Today salvation has come to this house!" There was a long silence.

"I just feel God has come to our house today", the husband quietly said.

All the work had been done by the brother's letter. God had created a hunger in their hearts. The Holy Spirit was drawing them to Jesus, challenging them to eat from the bread of life. A few hours later, Dave and I were sitting on a log trying to do our 'Ray Mears' bit. As we had left in the morning our 'Crocodile Dundee' friend had slapped a smoked Snapper fish on top of the rucksack. We were picking bones out of our teeth and trying to be grateful for our cold, fishy lunch, when, who should turn up, but our cafe owners. The very folk who had just accepted Jesus.

"We couldn't let you two guys go out in the rain without cooking you something." Out from the boot came some hot coffee and a steaming meat pie. God had provided!

Two jokers

"What are you two jokers doing? Trying to commit suicide?" asked the policeman. "You can park up that cross some place

and you can get in the motor and I'll take you to the next town."
The cross was hidden in the grass and we did as we were told,
after all, it was late in the evening, in fact, it was already pitch
black. Some truck driver had telephoned the police to complain
that he'd nearly hit us with his lorry. The good policeman had us
book in at a motel and early the next morning we hitched a lift
with a newspaper delivery guy to the place where we had left the
cross. After a few hours walking, we were back at the same motel
ordering breakfast.

Our waitress was fascinated by our trek across New Zealand. She
kept coming back to talk to us. "She's ready" said Dave," that
girl wants Jesus!"

I did a deal with God; "if she emerges from the kitchen when we
leave, I'll ask her if she wants to receive Jesus". Sure enough,
just as we were leaving, out she came, she even opened the
door for us and came outside to wish us goodbye.

"You want Jesus yourself, don't you?" said Dave. "Yes I do!" she
said, matter-of-factly. (There's no messing about with these New
Zealander's) She prayed, there and then, to commit her life to
Jesus, just outside the front entrance of the motel. Afterwards
she explained that she had been befriended by a great
Christian girl at school and she knew that she needed to make a
commitment.

Tears

On another occasion I witnessed to a young guy in his front garden. His brother had been 'bending his ear' about being born again but he had been very forceful about the matter, and the young man now had his barriers up.

Just then 'Dougie', an old mate of mine arrived on his motorbike. He used to preach on the tubes with me and now helped at a Bible College in New Zealand. He had come that day to walk and pray with us.

"Tell your story Dougie, about how you met Jesus!" I urged, as Dougie took off his motorbike helmet.

He then began to recount, how he had been running from the British police and had gone to Holland. "I was still well into my drugs at that time" he continued. Dougie began to choke up and cry as he recalled his sinful, druggie life. However, in Holland an ex-mercenary solider had picked him up when he was hitchhiking. The soldier had found Jesus and shared his story with Doug. To this day, that soldier doesn't know that after he had dropped him off and sped away, Dougie had got down on his knees at the side of the road and given his life to Jesus. Dougie's face shone as he shared his story and tearfully urged the young man in the garden to receive Jesus. The guy was now ready and he and his wife accepted the Lord.

The challenge

There were days when I couldn't understand it. We would spend the whole day in New Zealand meeting next to no one, and then the first person we would meet had clearly been sent to us. Often our job as an evangelist is simply to do what Billy Graham would do, he would present the gospel and then present **a challenge**. He famously would say "I want you to come down out of your seats to the front." The very act of leaving their seat acted as a demonstration of faith.

I recall having a ridiculously short conversation with a young man, towards the end of our walk in New Zealand. It went something like this:

"Do you know Jesus mate?"   "No!" he replied.

"Would you like to know Jesus?"   "Yes!" he replied.

"Let's prayer this prayer together! You can repeat it after me, but you've got to mean it for yourself!" I said, bowing my head.

At that point the young man prayed the simple prayer to receive Jesus. He was so sincere and deliberate as he prayed. But was it real? I asked him why he was so quick to pray with me. The whole conversation had only lasted two minutes and that was including the time spent praying.

"Well", he said thoughtfully, "I've got quite a few friends who are born again Christians and they've been telling me all about it. When you asked me if I'd like to know Jesus, I thought, well yes I do."

The reason why some people don't give their lives to Jesus is that they have never been asked. Apples come off the tree easily when they are ready to be plucked.

In Italy, I prayed with an Austrian guy who lived in South Africa. He lived with his friend who had been taking him to a German church in South Africa and had clearly been witnessing to him. Within minutes I sensed that the Austrian was at a crossroads in his life and told him so. "Will you give your life to Jesus right now?" I urged. There then followed a very long, pregnant silence. I was praying hard, under my breath while this guy just stared back at me, not saying a word.

To our joy, he eventually slowly nodded his head, saying yes to Jesus. I implored him to contact his South African friend to tell him of his decision. Sometimes the very act of telling someone your decision is a way of showing God that you mean business. "If you confess with your mouth that Jesus is Lord and believe in your heart that God raised Him from the dead, you will be saved. For it is by believing in your heart that you are made right with God and it is by confessing with your mouth that you are saved." (Romans Chapter 10 v 9-10).

Often I tell people that before we turn to Jesus, we are facing away from God, we are totally 'doing our own thing. I illustrate this, by standing with my back to the person (as if, for that moment, the person is taking the role of God.) I go on to say that, Jesus often used only a few words to call His disciples, saying just….. "Follow Me!" They did, they turned 180 degrees to face Him and as He walked away, they followed Him. I usually act this out physically, turning myself around 180 degrees to face 'God' and proceed to shake 'God's' hand. When seen acted out physically, it sometimes helps people to see how simple, yet profound the transaction between God and man can be. We just have to turn our self around and follow Him!

It seems at times, that 'all hell breaks loose' just as a person is about to pray to accept Jesus. A friend may turn up, the telephone may ring, all sorts of distractions kick in. I often tell the person that the devil is sending people along to stop them making the commitment. I have been known to request that their friend wait a few minutes while we pray.

Is it necessary for you to ask someone to pray out loud?

I would say "No, but it helps!" The sinner's prayer is not a formula, not a ritual or a magic mantra. It is simply a transaction by a person who simply wishes to say "yes". "Yes I want Jesus", "Yes I ask for forgiveness", "Yes I receive forgiveness", "Yes I want to change", "and Yes I ask Jesus into my heart to take control of my life".

Some people meet Jesus even without praying a set prayer. My friend, Dave, had been witnessing to Mark, his car mechanic, over the years, often mentioning about our trips abroad with the cross. Mark began asking so many questions that it was suggested that we all meet up together to talk.

We all gave our stories of how we met Jesus and eventually I asked Mark if he also wanted to pray to accept Jesus into his own heart. "I'll have to think about it!" he replied. This is the response that many make who are not ready, there and then, to make a commitment. Many say to me that they will pray when they get home. However, in my experience it often seems that when they put off doing it there and then, the devil is happy to keep distracting them from ever receiving Jesus.

However, the next day, Dave received a text asking "What's the prayer I have to pray, to accept God?" Before we could text back Dave received a telephone call from an excited Mark. He had gone to test drive a car and stopped at a beauty stop on the cliffs overlooking the sea. He was hungry for God and found himself saying "God, I want to be a Christian!" He said it again, only louder this time. Before long he was shouting it to God, "I want to be a Christian!" What happened then can only be from God. The car was filled with the presence of God. Mark felt the presence of the Holy Spirit touching his head, flowing through his body. His left hand began shaking. It felt as though God had placed His loving hands around Mark's heart. When I saw Mark a few days later his eyes were shining with that light that I often see in the eyes of Christians.

His wife gave her life to Jesus also and they meet once a week with my mate, Dave and his wife, Sandra to study the Bible. He hadn't prayed a formula but had said 'yes to Jesus'. Jesus was now his Lord.

By making Jesus our Lord we are asking Jesus to become our driving instructor. Instead of steering our life ourselves, we are allowing Him to give us directions. Sure, we can disobey His promptings and end up driving the wrong way around roundabouts, or even jump a red light or two but we usually come to realise that His ways are better than ours.

Another way we can look at it is that we become an *apprentice to Jesus*. He is the Master Craftsman and we are seeking to copy Him, following His example.

Is the person saved once they say the prayer?

When someone prayed to accept Jesus years ago, Christians would say that the person had just got 'saved'. "How many got saved tonight?" Christians would ask me after a night of evangelising. "How did you get on, did he get saved?" I have barely got out of earshot of the guy that I have been talking to, when some enthusiastic Christian asks that question. It is so embarrassing! Spitfire pilots would put a little Nazi swastika under their cockpit every time they shot down a German plane. Indians would carry the scalps of their victims on their belt. People are not notches or scalps; they are people who deserve respect. Jesus always showed the uttermost respect towards individuals who came to Him. To answer the question, we often don't know the depth of commitment that is made when people pray with us. Only God knows if they've 'got saved' or not because He can read their heart. Our job, however, is to encourage people not just to make a one off prayer of commitment but to turn their prayer into reality, to truly be a disciple of Jesus.

"Therefore, go and make disciples of all nations." said Jesus (Matthew Chapter 28 v19)

Sometimes, we might never actually see the person become a disciple. Maybe I've just prayed with someone to make a commitment and their bus has arrived or their friend has turned up and it hasn't been possible to talk any further.

I sometimes meet people who have told me that I had talked to them in the past but it wasn't until years later that they went on to give their lives to Jesus.

One such guy is now a Church of England vicar. The Reverend Keith Hitchman had been messing around with drugs at school and his headmaster said to me, "If you can do anything for young Hitchman, then good luck to you!" All I did for 'young Hitchman' was to talk to him about Jesus. It was the Holy Spirit who did the work and others helped him to grow in his walk with Jesus.

Although it is impossible to push anyone into making a commitment for Jesus, I am passionate about them making a decision. Where I can see that the Holy Spirit is clearly working with the individual, I will fight hard with all my might to encourage them to make a decision.

I remember talking regularly with one young lad who seemed to like listening to me talking about God and could actually see that he needed to give his life to Jesus. He was cheeky and always up to mischief. I'd see him doing 'wheelies' on his motorbike just in front of a police car and then enjoy the ensuing chase that followed.

"When are you going to give your life to Jesus?" I'd say, each time we met. He'd smile and reply "I'll think about it Lind's, honest." Then he would shoot off on his little motorbike. The day came when I visited the local nightclub only to find the young man's friends in a terrible state. "Had I heard the news?" they asked. It turned out that my young friend had shot off to buy pizza, driven too fast and, losing control of his car, had been instantly killed. I felt a new sense of urgency to encourage people to get themselves right with God.

Immediate Aftercare

I usually show someone who has just prayed a prayer of commitment a few Bible verses to give them reassurance concerning what they have just done. One question I may ask them is, "Do you know now that you have eternal life?" I may then go on to show them the following verses:

"I have written to you who believe in the name of the Son of God, so that you may **know you have eternal life**."
(1 John Chapter 5 v13)

"And this is the way to have eternal life – **to know You** the only true God and Jesus Christ the one you sent to earth."
(John Chapter 17 v3)

If the person has assurance that they have eternal life, I feel satisfied. I may then show them this verse:

"Jesus replied, 'I tell you the truth unless you are born again you cannot see the Kingdom of God.'"
(John chapter 3 v 3)

I then reassure them that they have been born again of the Spirit.

"But if we confess our sins to Him He is faithful and just to forgive our sins and to cleanse us from all wickedness."
(1 John chapter 1 v 9)

I then ask them if they believe that their sins are forgiven. This hopefully gives them an immediate awareness that they have made every attempt to get themselves right with God.

What if the person doesn't feel different?

Some people feel immediately different as a result of praying the prayer of commitment. They may feel God's presence and say that they feel peaceful and loved. One girl described it as having 'the Ready-Brek glow'. This is wonderful when this happens right from the start but it can sometimes leave them feeling bewildered when they wake up one morning and the honeymoon is over, they can't feel God's presence any more. I usually encourage the new Christians to see this as a compliment from God. God sees that they are now strong enough to follow Him by faith, not just by being dependent on strong feelings.

However, often people tell me that they didn't **feel** any different when they first prayed. I point out that nevertheless, they have made a decision to follow Jesus and that it may well be that later they will have a strong encounter of actually feeling the Holy Spirit. I have heard of wonderful Christians who have never felt the presence of God, yet have followed Jesus all their life. This truly, is living by faith and not relying on feelings.

Some tell me that it wasn't until months after the first prayer of commitment, that they really meant business with God and truly understood what it meant to have given their life to God. In every case I stress to the new Christian that following Jesus is a journey that ends up in heaven and I go on to encourage them to trust the truth of the Bible, rather just to rely on their feelings.

Before leaving people I usually ask them if they mind me praying over them again. (I tell them that they don't have to repeat this prayer but I am going to ask Jesus to really fill them to overflowing with the Holy Spirit.) I may then pray that they may sense God's closeness and know a real joy, that they may be protected from evil, etc. I am never really sure exactly what I pray but tend to just pour out my heart in prayer for them. I just let the Spirit lead me!

Sometimes I may pray softly in tongues for them as well. Although it may be thought that such a new language may alarm people, I have never found that to be the case. This is probably because the Holy Spirit usually speaks through me with such gentleness and softness that people generally feel loved more than anything.

Some have been intrigued and have asked what language I was speaking in. One man thought that I could speak fluent Hebrew. In Nepal, Dave and I were praying with a lady at the side of the road, and suddenly realised, that she was praying exactly the same as myself, word for word, every inflection. I cannot speak any more than a few words in Nepali and can only assume that I was speaking in tongues in her native Nepali language. Recently I was praying for a Christian in Assam, India who had told me that he often felt the devil attack him when going through the jungle. As I prayed for him in tongues the man became very excited asking how I knew his language. Apparently I had said, in his own language, "the devil has left, the devil has left!" This greatly encouraged my faith because I hardly knew a word of his language. Whatever your personal view on speaking in tongues or 'the fullness of the Spirit', my rule of thumb is that a true work of the Spirit always encourages, builds up and creates a comfort to the new believer.

Touch

I would see myself generally as a very tactile person. I make a point of shaking people's hands when I carry the cross. Touch can break down barriers. It is interesting that people who are antagonistic towards Jesus invariably refuse to shake my hand. However, most people reach out their hands when I reach out to them. I hope I have an attitude that seeks to love everyone so that, as I walk down a street, people see that I am out to greet everyone. As mentioned before, shaking hands has the added advantage of stopping people long enough for me to say just a few words to them.

In Bangladesh and other Asian countries I will hold a man's hand next to my heart as I pray with them. I have placed my hand on their heads as I pray prayers of blessing and hugged them afterwards. At the very least, they know that I love them and one thing I have learnt over the last twenty years or so of carrying the cross, *love is the universal language.*

One word of wisdom concerning touch - we must respect the personal preferences of people. Some people give off 'don't touch me' vibes, in which case for heaven's sake don't touch them. I am far more sensitive about this now and especially so, when speaking with women. A woman who has suffered abuse from a man may feel terrified or, at least very uncomfortable when a stranger invades their personal space.

In our country at this present time, we are also living in a culture of fear of abuse. For example, taking a young person down a dark alley or behind a bush in order to pray for them is asking for trouble! In fact, it is wise to avoid any situation where people could make accusation. To be accused (even falsely) in this area could close down your whole ministry and, should you work for a particular organisation, it can have a knock on affect on a far larger scale. Great care is needed here and the street evangelist is particularly at risk since he or she often finds them self working on their own.

My advice would be never to pray with a vulnerable person out of sight of others. I know this is not always possible but it is so important in today's climate. Further more, holding a teenager's hand or even laying hands on their shoulder whilst praying for them could be construed as abuse in this country. I personally think things have gone 'over the top' in our society's fear or even' phobia' on this issue but you would be foolish not to be sensitive to the climate in which we work.

Although this has not happened to me there are workers who have been accused of abuse. Although the allegations might have been unfounded, the old saying that 'mud sticks' is still true today. I think I understand that, even if an investigation is found to be proven untrue, a record of the investigation is still kept on file at the CRB records agency. I am sure that the devil is itching to shut down the work of any street evangelist (who may have had the most innocent of intentions in helping a vulnerable young person). Remember that damaged people can quickly turn from being friends into vicious enemies if they have felt hurt or rejected by you. They might not be averse to making false accusations against you. As stated before, a street evangelist does not work in a squeaky clean, sterile environment and this is another reason for working, if possible two by two and with female workers at hand for support.

Your baby

An adult may be happy to give their mobile telephone number. However, here again you have to be careful about taking the mobile number or address of a teenager. Unless you are part of an official street outreach organisation such as 'street pastors' the public may be very suspicious of your motives for having a teenager's contact details on your telephone. The most blame free solution is to give the person a neutral number such as that of a church. You can invite them to leave a message for you and assure them you will definitely get back to them. If you telephone them from the church, this will keep matters in the domain of the church and it is a better way of operating rather than giving out personal numbers to strangers. We also need to be mindful of protecting our family from nuisance calls or from being subject to any kind of harassment.

I have always found that, if a person is shy of coming to church, then it is best to arrange to meet them again at a neutral venue, i.e. McDonalds, KFC, Costa Coffee, etc. It is so important that you keep that appointment. *They* may not keep it (this happens a lot) *but we must always try to be reliable ourselves.* On countless occasions I have had a wonderful time with someone who has prayed to accept the Lord and has even promised to come to church but at the last moment they have chickened out. Don't allow this initial problem to discourage you, get in touch with them again. It is so important that you re-contact them. Even just seeing you can relight the spark. People have told me that just seeing me again has made them think about God.

We have to realise that the devil doesn't let go easily and will always try to frustrate any plans for the new Christian to become part of the church. Generally speaking, no news is rarely good news. If they have stopped contacting you, they may be struggling in their walk with God. Although this is not usually the case, there are exceptions where people go on wonderfully with God despite no other contact from other Christians. For example, I know of one Swiss woman who heard the gospel preached in her village. She accepted Jesus as her Lord but her husband at that time, wouldn't let her go to a lively church. She read her Bible and began trusting Jesus to help her in every situation. On one occasion she had to guide her cows up to higher pastures on her own. She had not done this on her own; normally the whole family would do this together (Otherwise the cows could go everywhere). She prayed and both she and the cows were led to higher ground by a bright light. Although she did not have contact with other Christians for many months, she grew in her relationship with God so much so that her husband, a mountain guide, gave his life to Jesus. When my first wife and I met her she talked of miracles as common place. She turned to us and asked us what miracles we had experienced. We felt so embarrassed to admit that we didn't have any such amazing stories to report.

Although not every church is good at receiving new Christians, (some churches could, if anything dampen the faith and enthusiasm of some young Christians), I believe that becoming part of a church fellowship is a God given concept. While God does look after Christians who cannot find a fellowship, the Bible makes it clear that Christians are part of an organism, a body, a family which should be effective in caring for the new Christians.

"So it is with Christ's body. We are many parts
of one body and we all belong to each other."
(Romans Chapter 12 v 5)

"And let us not neglect our meeting together as some people
do but encourage one another, especially now that the day of
His return is drawing near." (Hebrews Chapter 10 v 25)

CHAPTER 5

DRIVING LESSONS OUTSIDE THE CLASSROOM

Fishermen and shepherds
Street church in the making
Lessons and mistakes and the need for wisdom

Fishermen and shepherds

What can we do to help our new Christian to become part of God's church? It has been said that we Christians are the only Bible that some people read. If we pray with someone to accept Jesus, then we have acted as a 'midwife' to them. However, midwives are not necessarily foster parents who bring up the babies themselves. Midwives are around at the birth and naturally want to hand on the healthcare of their baby to other professionals, i.e. health visitors, paediatricians etc. In the same way the street evangelist does not necessarily always want to be a long-term pastor. However, the job of the street evangelist should always be to introduce a new Christian to someone with a pastor's heart.

Evangelists often tend to be pioneer types. They are hunters, fisherman, salesman, lifeboat men seeking more souls. Once they have "landed a catch" they are eager to go out again and find others. Pastors tend to be settler types; farmers, shepherds who want to care for their sheep and see them grow to maturity. In an ideal world we should have pastors working hand-in-hand with evangelists, both enjoying the gifting of one another.

The pastor's main concern is often to take responsibility for his church. This is his priority. Especially in a big church, pastors can find themselves becoming something of a 'business executive director'. Such a pastor may find it hard to be able to identify with or even understand the world of the street evangelist. Indeed, they may view the evangelist as a slightly eccentric character. I have been called 'a maverick' or a 'loose cannon'. I could be seen as someone who is more at home on the streets than in the church. When the street evangelist does attend church services he sometimes brings with him 'problem people' who don't always fit neatly into the church structures. They are not part of the 'golf club' and don't play the church game very easily.

On the positive side, I have invited some new Christians to church and they have often loved the service. They have found it to be like a 'Jacuzzi of God's love'. Some have found the music great and have felt God's presence during the times of singing. I have found that some pastors have a great way of explaining the Bible and are so gifted in helping the new Christians to grow in understanding. However, this doesn't always happen and for this reason it has been known that the street evangelist has found that they have had to end up running their own group in their own home or in a café or pub.

Street church in the making

Should the evangelist find himself starting such a group he may find that, as the group grows, then what may have started out simply as a 'nurture group', can end up feeling more like a street church. Those who attend can be reluctant to go to formal church because they have formed a relationship of trust with the evangelist. I have heard some new Christians complain that they feel judged in a 'straight' church. Even the liveliest of churches can feel very strange to someone from a different 'tribe'. Some have told me that while they may like the singing, they find the sermons very boring and heavy. They are not used to sitting through, something which, for them, feels like a university lecture. In a nut shell, it is sometimes not that easy to mix straight church with street church!

However, despite these difficulties, I believe that the established church should fully back the work of the street evangelist. It may be that the church will not see 'bums on seats' but needs to trust that street evangelism is an outreach to another 'tribe'. For example, I could imagine that converted Red Indians in America may have had their own way of worshipping Jesus which might have involved dancing around a camp fire. Similarly people who accept Jesus on the street may feel more comfortable in a less formal setting, than in a church service.

One young man who made a decision for Jesus at our local college began visiting my home and although from a children's home background felt accepted by my family. He eventually began bringing his friends along to visit us. At the same time a couple of guys from a drink/drugs background made decisions for Jesus. They had tried, not too successfully, to fit into a local church and so their pastor suggested that they visited the fledging group that had started to gather at my house.

Roughly about the same time another guy named Chris accepted Jesus. I had tried witnessing to Chris at the local nightclub but he made an excuse to go to the toilet once I had challenged him to ask Jesus to forgive his sins.

"Just got talking to some Bible basher bloke," he said to Anthony, one of his mates standing at the bar. Unbeknown to Chris, his friend Anthony had recently also given his life to Jesus. To Chris's surprise his friend ended up sticking up for me. The evening wore on and Chris asked his friend for a lift home when the nightclub closed. On the way home the two men began to talk about Jesus. By 5am, when it was getting light, they were still talking and before long Chris was giving his heart to the Lord. He began attending our little home meeting, bringing with him his two sisters who also made commitments. At the same time a friend of mine gave a lift to a guy who had a heavy drink habit and, after witnessing to him, brought him to our new group.

Suddenly there was a potential church in the making. I never meant to start a church or even wanted to start a church. I hate organising or leading and quickly looked around for someone who knew what they were doing to take over. A trainee minister said he would help but we soon discovered that both of us really didn't have a clue of what we were supposed to do with our new Christians. I quickly read studies prepared by organisations such as 'Agape' or 'The Navigators' and quickly threw together some teaching material. The Alpha course didn't exist in those days.

At our first proper meeting we went over the basics; what it meant to be born again, what it meant to be forgiven, what it means to make Jesus our Lord, etc. Then we tried studying subjects like prayer or the Bible. Everyone who attended was totally 'un-churched'. They couldn't easily look up Bible verses and most couldn't concentrate for any length of time, often disappearing outside every so often for a 'fag break'.

Heavy duty Bible study just didn't work. They weren't into listening to long talks. However, what did seem to work was teaching that included a liberal use of practical illustrations from our own life. Once the new Christians felt confident to ask questions or to contribute their own understanding on matters, the whole thing took off. The most successful form of Bible study was when we went through one of the gospels starting with Mark's gospel paragraph by paragraph. We just then discussed how to apply the teachings in our own life. As long as they were mostly doing the talking we were on a winner.

One long haired biker who was well into his cannabis would sit at the back looking bored every week. His girlfriend, however, was full of the Holy Spirit; she had obviously made the boyfriend come to the group. One day her boyfriend actually spoke. In fact, he looked different, more open and friendly, wearing a quick smile on his face. "What's going on here?" I thought. Sure enough, there had been a change! A big one! He had gone to hear Billy Graham preach in London and had given his life to Jesus.

I would try to encourage the group to attend our church, which was both lively and loving. However, somehow they seemed to enjoy meeting at our house where there was a sense of belonging. They could go out for their 'fag breaks', or they could make a fuss of our Alsatian dog who would sprawl himself out under their feet. People would sit up the stairs, on the floor, in the hallways and you would have to clamber over many bodies if you wanted to go the toilet. While coffee was being made in the kitchen people would ask to get prayed for and amongst dishes and pots and pans, prayers were offered, either for them to give their hearts to Jesus or to be filled with the Spirit.

Most knew brokenness and rejection in their life and appreciated the feeling of acceptance in our tiny house. To me these guys were our babies and their names were presented to God each day. They became our friends and they came out witnessing with me.

"I thought you'd come to beat me up." said one unsuspecting teenager as a bunch of these new Christians all dressed in leather biker jackets approached him

One young girl got touched wonderfully by the Holy Spirit as we prayed for her outside a burnt out store in town. "Oh it's so beautiful." she kept on saying as the Spirit fell on her. Soon the Spirit's work on the street proved God's reality to the group. They were being discipled, not in a classroom situation but out there in the real world.

Lessons, mistakes and the need for wisdom

I have made mistakes. I am sure I have talked too much. One guy once asked me if I ever talked about anything else other than about Jesus. At times, I have been far too intense. Hopefully, I would be far more laid back now. I remember being angry with one of them for sleeping with one of the most Spirit filled girls in the group. Since going out with him she had lost her fervour for God. My disapproval of their relationship was taken by the young man as rejection and I was seen as 'public enemy number one'. He never came back to the group again and perhaps lost his faith.

In my attempt to disciple these guys I took them into one of the schools with me. The only trouble was; it was one of those upmarket private girls' schools and the headmistress wasn't too happy about having ex-drug takers perhaps teaching her students things that weren't on the curriculum! More alarming was that the girls were more interested in the boys than what they had to say about Jesus.

On another occasion we all decided to go witnessing in a pub forgetting that one of them had a drink problem. The inevitable happened and we ended up having to take him home drunk. Most of us have undercover sins and fail secretly. For these guys they had more obvious sins. They may get touched by the Holy Spirit on Sunday and yet be 'out of their heads on drugs' on Monday. One guy (who thought the world of me when sober) hit me while he was drunk. He was so ashamed afterwards and couldn't believe he had done it. I did! I had the bruise to show for it!

"I became a Christian because Lindsay ..." My ears pricked up because I thought that the young man was going to give me some praise for explaining the gospel to him. I was a bit confused when he went on to say; "I became a Christian because Lindsay......... let me play with his Alsatian dog!" "What's my dog got to do with it?" I thought. The young man went on to explain that, coming from a children's home background few people trusted him but I had allowed him to care for my dog. This had impressed him sufficiently to make him want to search for Jesus.

I have always found that such new Christians are most effective on the street. If they have lived on the streets, they minister best on the streets. My friend Anita Hydes would work with me on the streets where she'd share her story about her deliverance from drugs. "Hello!" she'd say with a strong East End of London accent. "My name's Anita and I am a bad girl and 'ere's me old mate Lindsay, and he's a good boy!" People would be laughing and off we would go sharing our very different stories of how we met Jesus.

My great friend, Angie Taylor, walked with me with the cross from London to Brighton in memory of her teenage son, Shay. Shay had died at the age of eighteen only weeks before. He had set his heart on carrying the cross around all the seaside towns but sadly was killed in an accident at work before he was able to fulfil his ambition. His mother, Angie, had been a prostitute, alcoholic and 'bag lady', the lot. She had been raped in the past and even stabbed by a patient whilst in hospital. What a story! Yet despite, or perhaps because of her past, she taught me what it meant to truly love on the streets. She would hug and caress drunken, homeless men, in fact; she did everything the professionals insist you mustn't do. The people on the street knew she loved them. She was real and the tears flowed in the eyes of many as we left. She later went on to walk from Land's End to John O'Groats with her own cross, praying specifically for God to heal broken marriages.

I have found that the broken often minister best to the broken. I have learnt so much about compassion and honesty from those friends of mine who have travelled to hell and back before finding Jesus.

It is worth saying that it is not always the best idea to ask a newly converted addict to share their story too early in a church setting. In one way it's good, because they may feel very loved and accepted by the church. In fact, they might even be made to feel something of a celebrity for a time with people putting them on a pedestal because of the amazing work of God that has taken place in their life. However, in another way such adulation can set them up to fail publicly. The devil loves people being put on a pedestal, he can see clearly to shoot them down. Pride comes before a fall and the ego boosting that they may receive for being touted around for their great story isn't always helpful. If they slip back to their drink or drugs they may feel like a failed hero. Their sense of shame may be so great that they may not be able is to show their face in church again.

One way of helping the church to be involved with a group of new Christians is perhaps to ask the new Christian not to come to church initially but rather to ask certain established Christians to attend the 'beginner's group' instead. I have asked conventional Christians to leave the comfort zone of their church setting and to come as a guest to the 'beginner's group' with a view to sharing their own story. I have found that this has worked well, even if the Christian was the straightest guy out. Maybe he was old enough to be their grandad. However, he would often go down really well as long as he stuck to his personal testimony and didn't attempt to preach. In that way we attempted to integrate the two different 'tribes'.

Recently I prayed with a young man to accept Jesus. He had already attended a youth club at a local Baptist church but hadn't made a commitment. Since then he had been to jail and was at the point of wanting to change when we met him. He was invited to church and to my surprise came both morning and evening. I pray that he will keep coming to church but I fear that unless he is 'discipled' on his own 'territory' he may not continue to attend.

Often it is best to visit new Christians at their home, going over Bible verses in their sitting room. Sometimes friends or family members end up joining in. However, some teenagers are embarrassed to have you meet their family and would rather meet in a pub or a cafe. Pubs can be great. To open up the Bible and begin a Bible study in your 'local' could pave the way for a possible 'church in the pub'. I've seen friends of the new Christian come up to the table to find out what is going on and be drawn into the Bible study immediately.

One of the difficulties of operating in a pub is of course alcohol, both if it is taken by the new Christian or by spectators. Some new Christians have told me that alcohol loosens their tongue so they can share their faith more easily. However, I would argue that it is best to be 'under the influence' of the Holy Spirit not the other type of spirits. People can get aggressive or silly when drunk. If the pub has a heavy duty atmosphere or plays loud music then it is not always the easiest of environments to work in.

Cafes or takeaways such as McDonalds or Burger King or

the like can be far easier, especially if they are big enough to 'swallow up' a small group in the crowded restaurant area. As long as you are buying coffee or burgers staff often don't realise that you are doing a Bible study with your group of new Christians. In fact, if you intend to continue this type of ministry it is worth the management knowing what you are doing. I tell them that I am a Christian youth worker seeking to help the youth of the town. The development of the Street Pastor programme is such an advantage here since the police, the local authorities and businessmen can see the advantage of these uniformed individuals. If managers know that in some way you are trying to help young people stay out of trouble they can be very supportive of your work.

In Orpington, my old pastor friend, John Pressdee, came with me to McDonalds sitting himself down in the corner of the restaurant. Before long young people were drawn to him. Some of his church young people would bring their friends over to meet him.

"'Ere can you explain the gospel to my mate?" said one young man to me in McDonalds. Before long the guy had accepted Jesus. Where was the best place to teach the Bible to that guy? In McDonalds!! The 'go' part of Jesus' instruction to "Go into the whole world" shouldn't necessarily have to turn into a 'come' once they find Jesus. We can go and make disciples in McDonalds! This is the natural meeting point for many young people. It may be that God's future church will include the 'church of McDonalds' or 'the church that meets at the White Hart' or the 'Dog and Gun'.

My hope is that while there can be a variety of expressions of church in a town, the established church will love and feed into such unofficial discipleship groups. The pastors, evangelists, prophets, etc need to embrace however the Holy Spirit is working. If Alpha groups are working embrace them. If testimony groups held in pubs and cafes work embrace that. God's church can be a 'church without walls'. Does it matter if the Holy Spirit is working as much in McDonalds as it is in the Anglican, Baptist, Methodist or charismatic church? The important thing is that we go and make disciples.

CHAPTER 6

REACHING OUT TO PEOPLE OF OTHER FAITHS

Speaking their language

Speaking their language

I have carried the cross in Muslim Bangladesh, Buddhist Sri Lanka and Hindu/Buddhist Nepal and Hindu/Moslem Assam, India. People have often been far more loving and responsive to me in these countries than in 'Christian Europe'. Many in those countries could not work out what I was doing with a 12 foot cross on my back. "What is it?" is the common question that I am greeted with. One man thought I was measuring the road with the wheel on the back of the cross.

As soon as the cross was bolted together in Bangladesh an instant crowd would gather. People were always happy for me to preach about the cross.

"It's the symbol of how much God loves us," I'd say, and go on to talk about 'Isa', their prophet (Jesus). I never ever insult Mohammad or the Muslim religion but focus on the goodness of God, the Creator and the beauty of Jesus.

I realised, during my time in Bangladesh that I had to be wise in how I presented the gospel. Certain phrases could cause problems to a Muslim audience if worded in a certain way. For example, if I immediately refer to Jesus as *the Son of God* then I may lose my audience even before I am able to say too much at all. I asked the Lord for help and the phrase 'the Holy One of God' came into my mind.

Muslims find it offensive to think that Allah had sex with Mary but by using the phrase 'the Holy One of God' it has enabled me to go on to explain that *all of God was in Isa'*. He was the God/ man, the bridge between God and man. He was the perfect man, totally without sin! The one who possessed the Holy Spirit without limit! In more private talks afterwards it has then been possible to have the time to explain the meaning behind the term 'Son of God'. In the same way, some Muslims think that the Father, Son and Holy Spirit are three Gods so it is important to explain that God can show Himself in three different ways but there is only one God. I understand that there is a teaching in Islam that maintains that Isa (Jesus) didn't die. I gather it is thought that he was substituted, at the last minute by another who looked like Jesus. While I have been preaching I have pointed out that it is understandable for people to have thought that Jesus did not die because, after three days, He came back to life again. I have found myself saying something along these lines:

" Yes, humans could seek to kill His body on the cross (indeed they did, for blood and water had flowed out when the soldier stabbed His side) but it wasn't possible to get rid of the Holy One of God and three days later Isa burst out of the grave!"

Some may take issue with my thinking here saying that I am playing with words. There is no way I will water down the truth. I firmly believe that Jesus is the Son of God and will seek to help Moslems to understand this but where there are areas of difficulties for Moslems these can often be best explained in a more personal setting. Sometimes I have found that certain personalities in the crowd can wish to be contentious and where the crowd is volatile it very important to exercise wisdom.

I met a very studious son of a 'Mullah' (a Muslim priest/ teacher). He was insistent that I come to his house to meet his father. He was so fascinated by Jesus and he would often telephone us to ask us if we had got an Injeel (Gospel) for him. He had gone on before us, to his home town, to tell his friends we were coming. On arrival in his town we were immediately ushered into a restaurant and were joined by a group of young men who spoke perfect English. We talked in depth about the way of salvation. Suddenly one of them presented Dave and I with roses.

On leaving the restaurant, I found myself on my own waiting to move off with the cross, still clutching the rose. The inevitable crowd began to grow, staring at me holding the rose. I wasn't expecting to preach but suddenly the stunning sentence of a worship song sprang into my mind. "The Darling of heaven crucified." At that point my translator joined me and I began to preach about 'the most beautiful Man that had ever lived'. I felt so full of the Holy Spirit, I was trembling all over. As I held the rose high above my head and talked of how Satan tried to crush Jesus an incredible hush came over the crowd. It was a holy moment!

"Heaven held its breath, as drops of blood fell to the floor to cleanse our sin ... yet the Holy One of God could not be crushed! Three days later He rose, conquering death!" Fortunately the stem of the rose had not been broken and shot back up.

"That same Isa is alive and wants to take over our lives and come into our hearts."

I finished by saying in Arabic "Praise the Lord". I said it louder and the crowd repeated it until they were chanting, not in anger, but in joy. Praise the Lord!

I always relied heavily on my translator friend who coached my preaching into terms that Muslims could relate to. He would use the word 'Allah' to describe the God of Abraham. I know this can upset some Christians who would say that Allah is a false god and that Jehovah or Yahweh is the one true God. If 'Allah' is the Muslim word for describing the Creator God, then we used it in order to seek to communicate the gospel in their language. For example, if I was trying to communicate to a Hindu I may use the word 'Brahman' to refer to the one ultimate God. We have to start where the person is. It does not diminish our faith by using terms like Allah or Brahman, even if the concepts differ from what we mean by God. I have heard people in Bangladesh describe me as a 'Muslim that follows Isa'. If the word 'Muslim' means; *someone who is submitted to God*, then I can see what they mean. As a follower of Isa I want to be totally submitted to God.

I often talk to the Muslims about 'Eid al-Adha' (Festival of Sacrifice). During this time, cows are sacrificed in memory of when Abraham was about to sacrifice his son. While I understand that Muslims believe that the son, in this instance is Ishmael and not Isaac, I don't get into that debate. What I do focus on, is that God sent what the Bangladeshi Moslem refers to as the 'Dumba', an animal, (a lamb) to take the sacrifice. I am then able to point out, that Isa is described in the Injeel as the 'Dumba' of God, that is; the 'lamb of God who takes away the world's sin'.

"The next day John saw Jesus coming towards him and said, 'Look! The Lamb of God who takes away the sin of the world!" (John chapter 1 v.29)

Muslims do have a strong awareness of *sin*, of *heaven and hell* and of *judgement*. When I preach to them I centre on the holiness of God and how He cannot even look at sin. I talk of our sins of adultery, dishonesty, selfishness and the corruption of the human heart. I have found Muslims to be far more receptive and aware of their sin than people in the West. They know that they are not righteous.

"We can pray five times a day, we can give money to the poor, we can even make the pilgrimage to Mecca but will this take away the stain of sin? The good news is that the blood of Isa is the only thing that will cleanse away the stain of sin."

I have often sensed the Holy Spirit's presence on the crowd

and have had the opportunity of leading them in a prayer both to confess their sin and to receive forgiveness through the blood of Isa.

There is a fear of God among many Muslims and I always stress that *God is merciful* and has made a way to provide a *merciful solution* to our problem of sin. He has created a way of forgiveness for those who are truly repentant of their sins.

I have also found that it is possible to show Bible verses to Muslims without it causing the embarrassment that is often found when the Bible is opened in the West. Indeed, in Asian countries there often appears to be a great respect for Holy Scriptures. One Asian air passenger was aghast to find that I had my Holy Bible in a bag at my feet in the plane.

The Injeel (The Gospels) is seen as 'the Evangel or Good News, the original Scriptures revealed to Jesus by God'. They also respect The Taurat (The first five books of the Old Testament) as the 'original Scriptures revealed by God to Moses'. Furthermore, they recognise The Zaboor (The Psalms) as Scripture revealed to the prophet David. The Qur'an teaches that all three, the Injeel, the Taurat and the Zaboor are '*guardians of the truth.*'

I will often let my Muslim friends know that I am aware of the above and will then go on to say "Let's look at what the Injeel has to say about Isa, your prophet." I may then show verses that illustrate the claims that Jesus make about Himself.

"I am the Way, the Truth and the Life, no one can get to the Father by means of me." (John Chapter 14 verse 6)

"I am and the Father are one." (John Chapter 10 verse 30)

"The absolute truth is that I was in existence before Abraham was ever born." (John Chapter 8 verse 58 Living Bible)

"I am the Good Shepherd. The Good Shepherd sacrifices His life for the sheep." (John Chapter 10 verse 11)

"I am the Resurrection and the Life, he who believes in Me, even though he dies like everyone else, shall live again. He is given eternal life for believing in Me and shall never perish." (John Chapter 11 verse 25 Living Bible)

Sometimes I might refer to the Old Testament, showing them Isaiah Chapter 53. They are usually happy to read the whole chapter.

"All we like sheep have gone astray. We have left God's path to follow our own, yet the Lord laid on Him the sins of us all." (Isaiah Chapter 53 verse 6)

Often the Muslim will realise that this passage is referring to 'Isa'. I might follow that with a verse such as 1 John Chapter 4 verse 10.

"This is real love, not that we loved God, but that He loved us and sent His Son as a sacrifice to take away our sins."

I am aware that some Muslims can be like nominal Christians in this country who may not know that much about their Faith. By learning a little about Islam it can help you communicate with a quiet authority. I have a great love for Muslims and want them to know that there can be an assurance of eternal life.

"I don't want you to go to hell, I want to see you go to heaven." I say whilst holding their hand.

What about the fear of violence?

Before going to Bangladesh to carry the cross I would feel fear. I would wake up at night and begin wondering if an extremist would shoot me. Was this going to be the last time I would see my loved ones? Jesus went through the same thing in the garden of Gethsemane but a thousand times worse. Soldiers have to go through this fear barrier as well. *"Face the fear and go anyway!"*

"And so dear brothers, I plead with you to give your bodies to God. Let them be a living sacrifice, holy the kind He can accept. When you think of all He has done for you is this too much to ask?" (Romans Chapter 12 verse 1. Living Bible)

The minder

Before we left for Bangladesh, my wife had a vision. In the vision she saw that I had sheltered under a large tree because of the heat. A large crowd had gathered and I had begun preaching, some were accepting everything I said, others were not. However, I didn't have to fear because an enormous angel was standing behind me overseeing everything.

Within a few days of the walk, that very event occurred. The crowd had gathered and a great joy came on me as I preached. I was aware that many were receiving what I said. However, as in the times of Jesus, there were also the 'teachers of the law' listening at the back. I could see heavy duty characters shaking their heads in disapproval. Was I in danger? I didn't care; I was so full of joy that even if a gun had been produced I would have cried out "Here I come Jesus!"

It was only when it was all over that I remembered Debbie's vision. I never saw the angel but I am sure he was there!

Some argue that it is easier to share Jesus with Hindus! "After all", they say "they will see Jesus as just one more god to add to the thousands they've got already." While I can see the logic, I have found that in Hindu areas there can be just as much of a spiritual battle going on! We have to realise that, behind every false god, there is a spiritual power, a demonic force. This came through very clearly in Nepal.

We had been having a fantastic time doling out thousands of Christian leaflets along an 8km stretch of the main Kathmandu to Pokhara highway. There was a traffic jam and everything had ground to a halt. As we made our way along the queue of lorries, buses, cars; everyone got a leaflet. The difference between Nepal and the UK is that, in Nepal people actually read leaflets. I was full of joy. I even got to preach to whole bus loads of people.

However, with lungs full of exhaust fumes we felt it was time to wash the dirt down our throats and stopped off at one of the tea-houses that line the road. Standing outside was a mother and her teenage daughter. The young girl was dressed in a red wedding dress. She could only have been about twelve years old. Deb had some small metal crosses that an American church had passed onto us and she placed one of these into the girl's palm as a 'wedding present'. I wasn't too sure what was going on and presumed that she was actually to be wed that day. However, we learnt that the girl's 'god' had told her to dress up in the dress as an act of worship, signifying her commitment to that 'god'.

As we talked with the girl Deb felt led to start singing worship songs. With no warning, the girl became hysterical, her beautiful face contorting as she shouted out angrily. As we prayed she calmed. I cannot say she accepted Jesus or that she found freedom from her spirit ruler. However, the incident did amply demonstrate the obvious clash of spiritual powers often experienced in Asia.

More recently we found ourselves sleeping outside a house of a simple farmer who had kindly shown us hospitality. During the evening friends of his had arrived to meet the 'Westerners'. Our translator had done a great job explaining our faith to them but was aware that some did not like what they had heard and wanted us to leave. The atmosphere deteriorated further when a Hindu 'Holy man' arrived; took drugs in front of us and began giggling in a strange way. Another man arrived who appeared to be very demonized. I ended up praying for him with an authority that certainly was not of me. This caused further consternation with some of the visitors and by the time we bedded down we felt very vulnerable to say the least.

My two mates Dave and Edward fell to sleep and I asked the Lord to keep me awake to keep guard. My host kindly decided to 'keep guard' as well and made up a sleeping area next to me. However as he did this he began to sing worship songs to Krishna and to Vishnu (Hindu gods). He also began giggling. It seemed like the spirits were seeking to mock us through him. I knew he spoke no English. It was therefore somewhat disconcerting when he suddenly announced in perfect English; "You are not welcome here, we do not worship your God, you must leave our village". I began chiding myself for getting myself in this mess. I felt very responsible for deciding to stay in this dark place. My praying became very real and desperate as I imagined a mob of enraged Hindus arriving to drive us away. Thankfully my host fell to sleep but I was then confronted with his brother pestering me, insisting that I give him money. It was all becoming somewhat scary. In the end I laid my hand on the man's head and spoke in tongues. A beautiful prayer language came out of my mouth accompanied by the gentle atmosphere of the Living God. The man quickly became sleepy and caused no more trouble. In the morning I was grateful that the angry mob had never arrived and the atmosphere had changed for the better. We left the village in peace but also aware that very real forces had been at work seeking to intimidate us. We have spiritual protection with our Jesus but we should never take lightly that we are in a spiritual battle.

There are times when I have felt the atmosphere in some villages to be very volatile and have just known that, if I stay too long there is going to be trouble. My translator will quickly say "Let's go" and I rarely argue. This happened in one Moslem town in Assam. People would refuse to shake my hand or even look at me at times. I was relieved to leave the place and yet in another Moslem village days later, everyone lined the streets to greet us. There was a spirit of praise on the crowd and all I could do was wave and shout "praise Jesus, praise God". I felt like a surfer being carried along by a strong wave of worship and praise of God. People, perhaps without realising it, were praising the unseen Jesus who was walking ahead of us. When we met the village elders they rubbed perfume on us and embraced us in a wonderful loving way. Praise invokes the power and beauty of our wonderful God. When faced with fear and intimidation, start praising! A power is activated as you lift your eyes towards heaven and start worshipping and praising.

The loving man who crossed a bridge

We had just crossed a bridge and entered into a Nepali town. It was 'Devali week' (the Hindu Festival of Lights); something similar to Christmas week for us Christians. The alcohol had been flowing and crowds pressed in to watch a fight between two men.

I tried preaching to the crowd to distract them but the fight was far more exciting than a little English preacher with a big cross! I had to try different tactics. Standing at the other side of the road I attempted to sing a Christian worship song at the top of my voice. The crowd was even less impressed at the rendition and again turned back to watch the fight.

However, to my surprise, all the kids began to run over excitedly and gathered round me. "I'm going to tell you a bedtime story!" I had no idea what I was going to say but I was committed now. The gorgeous kids looked at me with such love and expectancy that I had to keep going. I found myself telling them about 'the strange man' who one day walked over the bridge and into their village. To start with the kids thought I was talking about myself but, as the story developed, it became clear that the man in the story wasn't me but Jesus who had been sent into a world of people fighting each other.

"The adults ignored Him and kept fighting but the children loved him and kept climbing on His knee."

By this time, the children's parents had come to listen as well. A hush came over the crowd. The Holy Spirit was there. A 'magic moment'!

I eventually gently invited the youngsters to kneel with me to receive Jesus. It was such a beautiful, peaceful scene; children kneeling, praying, thanking Jesus for dying for them.

Suddenly, 'all hell broke loose'. A screaming Hindu woman launched herself into the crowd of kids, driving them away. I lifted my head just in time to see children flying in all directions seeking to escape her wrath. "We are all Hindus. We are all Hindus" the 'screaming Banshee' raged hysterically. What was I to do?

Jesus took over! My translator Devendra placed himself right in front of her, meeting her aggression with absolute calm. In fact, his face began to positively shine.

"You will be the first in the village to come to Christ and you will find no peace until you go to church!" His voice was quiet, gentle and yet full of authority.

The crowd, who had now tired of their 'Devali-fight' crossed the road to watch 'God's firework display' On the one hand, they could see absolute peace emanating from Devendra, and yet on the other hand, anger and rage flaring from the eyes of the woman. Here was light and darkness opposing each other!

Within minutes, the woman seemed to lose her power. She skulked away into the crowd, still mumbling. I took the opportunity to shake hands with everyone, wishing God's peace (shanty) on one and all, including the 'hot headed fighters'. The day had been won by Jesus; the one who had come into a world full of anger and hatred; the one who sought to teach the world how to love!

I don't think the children will ever forget what happened in that town that day!

The supernatural boy

A very insistent twelve year old boy ordered us up to his house and began showing us the *tikka*, a red colouring applied to the forehead at Devali. I found myself telling him that I could explain what the tikka meant (I had no idea at that time what I was going to say).

Out of the blue came the thought that, in the Garden of Gethsemane, Jesus had sweated beads of blood on His forehead. I preached to the young boy at length, challenging him to ask Jesus for forgiveness and to accept His cleansing. He thought for a long time and then nodded that he wanted to give his life to Jesus.

Before he would allow us to leave he insisted on showing me the village's altars to Krishna and Shiva. I impressed upon him that he was now a follower of Jesus and that he no longer needed to worship these idols any more. I am not sure if he took this on board but before we parted he did insist on carrying our cross for 100 yards, a mighty feat for such a slight young boy. He appeared to have a very controlling nature but I pray that a significant work of God was done in him that morning.

Devali

The teenagers seemed to be having a great time; crowding in a circle they watched one of their female friends dancing to attract a male suitor. What beautiful, attractive young people, all cheering and egging on their friends to dance.

In the next moment, we were also waved into the circle to dance as well. We guys looked like Mick Jaggar on speed. The crowd were so loving to us and before long allowed us to say a few words about the *Light of the World* – Jesus. On other occasions we did a short drama sketch about Jesus healing our broken hearts. Everyone seemed to enjoy themselves and I could picture Jesus dancing with these lovable teenagers. We had such a great opportunity to witness for Him that morning, it took us half a day to get through the town and hundreds of teenagers heard the gospel.

When something just isn't right!

In one town I felt that I should erect the cross upright. A crowd gathered and I sought to preach my heart out to those listening. However, something wasn't working! Often I find freedom and inspiration and I am aware of the Holy Spirit giving me the words to say. (On these occasions I can't remember what I've said afterwards.) This time, however, I felt far from being anointed. It was like wading through treacle. I was even struggling to think of what to say next. My words felt like cardboard and I drew matters to a close quite quickly.

Before leaving we offered to pray for the sick and people came forward for healing. One or two appeared to have been touched by the Lord. However, it seemed that no one wanted to make an open confession of faith in Jesus. Deb had felt unable to sing happy praise songs and we wondered what we had done wrong. We had with us Jenny, a godly intercessor lady. She clearly felt that something very bad had happened in that town in the past and that the Lord had turned His face away from the people due to their disobedience. In this case, only songs of repentance were appropriate.

Other towns received the truth enthusiastically and I was shocked to find young people thanking me warmly for sharing the truth about Jesus. Many young people had Christian friends who were witnessing to them. These teenagers who strutted around trying to look so cool were often our greatest friends and appeared to drink in the gospel message. What an exciting country! If these teenagers really find Jesus the whole country could be affected.

Does your Hindu temple have a toilet?

Once, in Bangladesh, I found myself desperately needing the toilet. Asia and my weak stomach are not the best of friends.

"You must come to my Hindu Temple for a debate!" demanded a Hindu leader. I have no interest or time for debates. If people just want to argue I just shake their hand and move on. However, the man was insistent that we come to his temple and since my need for a toilet was desperate we risked death, crossing the main Dhaka- to-Chittagong highway to visit his temple.

(Although our main fear was of being attacked by Muslim extremists, I imagine that greater work for the angels was protecting us from being flattened by the dilapidated but highly decorated trucks and buses that throw themselves at each other with no thought of safety. Their drivers lean constantly on their horns to warn of impending danger. The Bengali guides would hold my hand and drag me across the road. Making it across was largely due to pure Adrenalin!)

I made it to the toilet, emerging to see a whole crowd gathered outside the temple. "Preach on the living water", a voice in my heart urged. The Holy Spirit was there and an old lady began jumping up and down excitedly as the gospel was preached. We began praying and people began asking for prayer for healing. They wanted Christians to return in the future and to bring with them a Bible. They were so hungry for God and we left as good friends. All things, including an upset tummy, can work together for good when God is in control!

In some ways, Hindus might appear more 'liberated' than Muslims. It would upset me, for instance, to see the look of fear or pain in the eyes of so many Muslim women in Bangladesh. Jesus was angry with the Pharisees for loading down heavy burdens on the ordinary people and over-strict religious legalism can create a climate of fear.

In Nepal, the Hindus didn't have a fear of the 'One Almighty God of Abraham'. However, they did know the fear of having to appease their own particular god. Both Muslims and Hindus have admitted to me that they have no assurance that they are going to heaven. My preaching, therefore, seeks to show them how they can know for certain that they have eternal life. A Hindu or Buddhist is hoping to be reborn and come back into a better state. A Hindu might be seeking to be enlightened in order to 'find the god that is within them'.

It is important to stress that Jesus came to make a way for us to escape from the circle of reincarnation. Being born again does not mean having to live one life after another until we get it right. Rather, it is receiving forgiveness and God's Spirit to empower us to life the new life in relationship with the living God.

I do not know everything about Asian religions but my time

in Bangladesh, Nepal Sri Lanka and India has shown me that the good news of Jesus actually reaches the deepest desires of a Muslim, Hindu or Buddhist. Jesus sets us free from the wheel of reincarnation and sets us free from the hard work and fear of having to obey laws to pacify your god and earn your salvation.

As I say, I rarely get into heavy debate and avoid getting into a battleship position whereby each party simple fires arguments at each other. However, I do try to use what I know of their religion to 'talk their language'. If I can show how Jesus can lead them into an intimate experience of knowing the one true living God, then I hope I have preached the good news successfully to them. The simple gospel has a power to reach anyone from any religion.

A Hindu might say 'all religions lead to God' but it has been said that *all religions lead to Christ*. 'Perfection'; the hope of Asian religions, can only be given by the 'perfect' i.e. by Jesus Christ. While Islam seeks God's truth and justice, both of these can be found in Jesus. Hindu scriptures, the Vidas, speak of the perfect sacrifice and again, this can be found in Jesus.

Much of my time, as I make my way through a country with the cross, is spent simply praying! This is as important as preaching! We have to cry out to the God of truth to set people free from the spirit of false teaching. Remember that so many false religions/cults have been started by a visitation of an angel (an evil spirit or demon). This demonic spirit can give experiences in order to tie people up in fear and deceive people from the truth. Prayer is the major weapon we have to counter such forces.

Armies on the hills

At one point, in the Nepal walk, both Deb and Jenny (the intercessor) had felt oppression coming against us. Deb had felt that her role wasn't so much to give out tracts but to walk ahead of the team worshipping in song with her guitar. (I felt the closeness of Jesus when she had done a similar thing in Sri Lanka.)

On this particular morning, Deb's singing became particularly strong and anointed of the Spirit. It was as if a new power had taken her over. Jenny joined us exclaiming, "Don't worry the armies of heaven are with us now!" Both Jenny and Debbie could sense the powerful presence of God. Deb at one point had seen the skies parting above the mountains and she sensed that heaven had opened its doors above Nepal. At the same time, Jenny had seen warrior armies stationed on the ridges of the mountains surrounding us. People had had similar visions and dreams both before and during the walk. Those looking with a natural eye sometimes underestimate the power of such a simple act of worship such as walking and praying through a country.

I have an American brother, Keith Wheeler, who carried

the cross along the same road in 1993 when there were few believers. Since then thousands of new believers have been added to the Nepali church and often we would hear the words "Hallelujah" from a believer as the cross went by.   Sometimes the Believer might be the only one in their family or in their Hindu village and they were so encouraged to pray with us.

I had a dream

"We have to have a cup of tea with this lady." urged Devendra my interpreter. "We can't have a cup of tea with everyone" I muttered "otherwise we will never get to Pokhara this year." I was silenced and shamed as Devendra started to explain that the woman was so excited because she had had a dream from God that a man carrying a big cross would come and pray for her. We prayed for her and her family as they were experiencing great struggles. Everyone matters and it is easy to lose sight of that in the process of a long distance walk. We have to remember that God loves the Asians and wants to reveal Himself to them.

CHAPTER 7

KEEP GOING

Something happens when I carry the cross
Keep preaching, Linds, keep preaching
Keeping going despite fearful thoughts
Resting in the Spirit
Keep going even if you blow it
Even if it seems nothing happens, something happens
You will get opposition

Man in the hole

As I knelt down to greet the man who was working down in the electrician's inspection chamber, his colleague began to laugh. The black guy, standing by the inspection chamber was making sure that the public were aware of the work going on beneath the pavement.

In the chamber, a white guy was fiddling with the underground wires. Being beneath ground level, he hadn't noticed that I was kneeling down quietly behind him. He turned around, saw me.

"Jesus!" he gasped. "No", I smiled "I'm not Jesus, I only work for Him." His black colleague, a Jamaican, thought this was a great reply and belly-laughed. I quickly explained what I was up to. I had just walked from London to Wolverhampton carrying the cross and was now only a stone's throw from the end of the walk at the city centre. I began to tell the underground electrician about Jesus.

"Jesus loves you so much, mate" I started.

"Dat's right!" boomed the Jamaican. "Dat's exactly what I've been telling him man!"

"He wants to come into your life so you can have His Spirit living in you." I went on.

"Dat's right! Ain't that what I've been telling you?" screeched the Jamaican, beaming all over his face. "I've been telling this to him, day after day."

"Sin is like a break in the electric wire, sin has got us disconnected to God but Jesus fixed it for us so that we can now be reconnected because He died on the cross" I continued, (trying to make it relevant to the job he was doing.) Before long it seemed plain that everything I said was making sense to the electrician.

"You know man", the big jovial black guy butted in "I've been telling this guy this stuff for ages now man." Turning to his friend he said "Ain't that right mate?" The guy nodded thoughtfully.

"Listen mate" I said gently to the electrician, "how would it be if your friend here led you in a simple prayer to invite Jesus to take over your life?" I turned to the black guy seeking his encouragement. The Jamaican was so happy he was almost jumping up and down with excitement.

It was decided that I should lead them in prayer and the Jamaican guy would join in for 'moral support'.

A 'prayer meeting' then took place with the electrician, the Jamaican and I huddled around the hole; the electrician standing, hands clasped together, in his inspection chamber. As I left, the Jamaican and I hugged each other like long lost brothers and I placed his newly born-again colleague in his care and completed the short distance into the town centre to end the walk. I was so encouraged; I didn't want to finish the walk. In fact I couldn't wait for the next walk with the cross. These walks are like a drug to me!

Something happens when I carry the cross that doesn't when I don't!

People ask me why I carry the cross! They say that, surely I can witness for Jesus without making a 'spectacle of myself'. Although I realise it may be that carrying the cross has become part of my identity I do not have any wish to draw attention to myself. I just want the attention to be on Jesus; people see the cross and usually immediately associate it with Him. As a result, within seconds we are talking about Jesus.

I don't really feel at home when someone, in their desire to help me, asks if I would let them carry the cross. Walking behind that person, trying to witness while they disappear around the corner with my cross sometimes causes me problems. I feel almost 'naked' without it on my shoulder.

For me the cross is a tool of the gospel that opens doors into people's hearts. Some people even get touched by just seeing it being carried!

In Bangladesh a young man looked out of the window of his bus and saw the cross being carried along at the side of the busy road. A 'strange feeling' came over the bus passenger and he knew he had to meet us. He got off as soon as possible, waited for a bus returning in the opposite direction and returned back to see us. He wanted to know what the 'strange feeling' was. Within a short time he had heard the gospel and received Jesus.

Two bits of wood bolted together brings out the lovers of

Jesus who often kiss me or shake my hand, thrilled to see the *symbol of our beloved Lord* being presented to the crowds. It also brings out the demonic, the scoffers, the intrigued and the amused. Light clashes with darkness as the cross is carried.

The naked man

At Glastonbury Rock Festival, I often saw the powerful effect of the cross! I remember trying to share the gospel with a whole bunch of tall, black Rastafarians. Usually I find that Rasta's are very easygoing but on this occasion at Glastonbury, a very intimidating spirit prevailed. In the corner of my eye I was aware that an old man had come to stand behind me. "See him off!" The Rasta appeared to be addressing the old man.
I turned to look more closely at the shadowy figure lurking behind me. I wasn't prepared for the sight that greeted my eyes! The man looked like a character in the Bible. His wrinkled face was ashen white. Long straggly hair hung on his shoulders. He was wrapped up in a flimsy white sheet. "A harmless eccentric!" I mused.

However, this 'harmless eccentric' turned out to be a nightmare operating under some strong spiritual power. As I tried to share Jesus with the festival-goers he constantly hassled me. At one point, he began shouting "Cross for sale, nails included!" This might have seemed amusing to onlookers but it appeared to trivialise everything I was trying to do. I was becoming more and more troubled by his antics.

With no warning, he suddenly leapt on me, wrestled the cross to the floor and sat on it. It was the cross he hated. I tried everything to try to get rid of him, *binding, loosing, commanding* - all in the name of Jesus. I even appealed to some police officers for help. This only provoked the mad man to shed his sheet and present a scrawny naked body to the female police officer. She gasped, covered her eyes, turned her back and fled.

By now I wasn't too sure what to do. In the end, I met another Christian and we prayed together against whatever was controlling the 'mad demoniac'. As we were praying the old man seemed to become confused and, to my relief, wandered into the crowd. That was the last I saw of the ancient 'wizard'. There is a spirit world!

To those who have been saved, the cross is attractive and draws people to God.

"And when I am lifted up from the earth I will draw everyone to Myself." (John Chapter 12 verse 32)

However, to those who are not being saved the cross can be offensive and they sometimes spit out the vilest curses against Jesus as the cross passes by.

I even had my original cross stolen in the middle of the night at Reading Rock Festival. The drunk who stole it walked past the night security guys claiming to be Jesus. The cross probably ended up on a camp fire. I was gutted. However, a friend of mine had built a cross for himself made out of Iroko, a heavy but durable wood known as 'poor man's teak'. This cross was substantially bigger than the first one; however, it is of far better quality with a 'bomb-proof' wheel. I have carried this 23 kilo cross now for the last 20 years. The cross seems to have grown and I seem to have shrunk. "I was 6 foot 5 inches when I started." I joke with enquirers. It measures 6ft by 12ft and splits into three for transport and travels as *sports equipment* on airlines. Customs officials spend a long time trying to work out what I'm up to with *'three bits of wood and wheel'* as my only 'main luggage'.

I was ill one year over the Glastonbury weekend and couldn't carry the cross until the last day and even then, I only had the strength to carry it for a few hours. "What a waste," I thought; feeling that absolutely nothing had been achieved that year.

However, during the following year's festival a young Christian shared with me that he had been at a very low point in his relationship with God the year before.

"I saw you carrying the cross and something happened inside of me and I gave my life back to Jesus." He then asked if he could have the privilege of carrying the cross.

What happened then was both scary and yet glorious. A madman suddenly grabbed the cross off my new friend. I have become very possessive about the cross, having had so many drunk guys 'help me' in the past. "I'm Simon ... let me lighten your load!" they'd say. They would then seek to create havoc by wrenching the cross off my shoulder. On one occasion a drunk launched himself at me causing the cross and the two of us to come crashing down on the festival goers. I was beside myself with anger at his stupidity.

Here was history repeating itself. I was understandably quite perturbed to see my cross disappearing in the distance carried by a mad demoniac bedecked with filthy jeans, German 'Para-boots' and stripped half naked, matted dreadlocks halfway down his back. He was sprinting up to the stone circle carrying the cross as if it was a matchstick. Off he went at full speed running around the stone circle which overlooks the whole festival. The crowds seemed strangely moved by the spectacle and when the madman collapsed in the centre of the stone circle I sensed that an eerie silence had fallen on the onlookers ... here was my chance to preach.

"What you've seen just now is an amazing declaration of the love of God for humanity. God has sent His Son to the world to die for us all. Just as this man has run around the circle with the cross, so God's love surrounds the world. He is calling on us to receive the love He offers."

I could have made more of the preach but, by now, the madman was back on his feet lifting the cross upright high above his head. With the cross weighing as much as it does it was clear that a supernatural strength had to be controlling the guy. I knew that if the cross fell on people, there was certainly going to be a fatality. I had to do something quickly.

Standing in front of him I stared into his eyes. Whether he was stoned or possessed, or both, I don't know but his eyes betrayed something quite animal-like. I put my hand on his head and prayed in tongues. There are no set of guidelines for situations like this. The only thing I had was prayer. As I prayed, gradually the rage inside the man subsided. I retrieved the cross and no one got killed that day and the man disappeared meekly into the crowd. "What was all that about?" I mused to myself, the adrenalin still pumping around my body.

When the Holy Spirit is at work I always find myself 'playing catch up', trying to understand what is going on.

I remember one year at the festival, suddenly being confronted with several dwarfs dancing around in front of me as I tried to make my way through the crowds with the cross. It was surreal! Where were they from? Were they a troupe of circus artists? They ran cackling back and forth before me like medieval jesters. I remember thinking that the whole scenario would have been very much at home in a Robin Hood film. Was this really happening?

"This man is a follower of the Most High God", one of the dwarfs shouted, "and he is announcing to you the way of salvation!"

It reminded me of the demon-possessed slave girl who

followed behind Paul and Silas shouting, "These men are servants of God and they have come to tell you how to have your sins forgiven." (Acts Chapter 16 verse 17 Living Bible)

Just then, a girl leapt at me in a wild state of frenzy, screaming, shaking and laughing. I told her why I was carrying the cross and she fell to her knees crying. I prayed for her. "You can't have her?" shouted one of the dwarfs. "She is a child of Beelzebub." The Holy Spirit was there and I felt the compassion and authority of Jesus. A joy came on me, calming my fear. A man baptised me with beer as I continued praying for the girl at my feet. "Jesus loves you, Jesus loves you" I whispered, my voice full of the gentleness of the Spirit. She seemed overwhelmed by the quiet truth that she was hearing.

Another young man shouted, "She's sold herself to satan."

Yet the Lord was seeking to rescue her from Satan's kingdom and bring her into the kingdom of the God. Suddenly the girl and the dwarfs disappeared into the crowds. I was left exhausted and stunned. It had all happened so quickly. I don't know what has happened to the girl but I believe that God did something very powerful in those few minutes. It was a *power encounter* with two forces fighting for the soul of that dear girl.

I recall on another occasion having what I can only describe as a 'stand off' with a witch as Glastonbury. This is something I would never seek to orchestrate. However, suddenly I was confronted with a woman who was clearly praying very hard over me and I sensed that she definitely wasn't a fellow Christian but served a very different god. There she stood, staring me in the eyes praying. I faced her, quietly praying in tongues under my breath. I didn't feel scared but very secure in my Jesus. After a minute or so she seemed to come out of her trance and reverted back to normality.

"You are incredibly strong!" she said as she made out to leave.

"No love" I said, "I've just got Jesus!"

There it is……. the powerful truth in four words! **"I've just got Jesus."** Sometimes these power encounters demonstrate just how much protection and authority exists through *just having Jesus!*

"Greater is He that is in you than he that is in the world." (1 John Ch 4 verse 4)

"All authority in heaven and earth is given to Me therefore go and make disciples in all nations." (Matthew Ch 28 verse 18-19a)

Jesus finishes His command by adding, "I am with you always even to the end of the world." (verse 20b)

I am not strong, anything but! However, I do have an incredibly strong Jesus who lives in my heart.

"Keep preaching, Linds, keep preaching!"

"If you died today, would you know for certain that you are going to heaven?"

People looked up, shocked that someone dared to speak publicly on the train. Immediately they buried their heads back into their newspaper once they realised it was just another annoying preacher. In the short time before the train pulled away I was able to say quite a bit. I realised that I wasn't following my usual style of preaching but was focussing on the urgency of getting ourselves right with God. I pointed out that we never know when our time is up. When I finished I felt a bit deflated. Had they taken in anything I said or had they written me off as a religious nutcase? Was it even worth embarrassing everybody with this sort of talk?

Within five minutes the train had gathered up speed. Suddenly the carriage lurched violently to one side, people gasped and I lost my balance grasping quickly for a handle to steady myself. Although the train did not derail, the incident was sufficient to shake us all. I saw my opportunity "There you are folks ... you never know when your time is up." People were not amused! I *was* a nutcase!

As I got off the train at Streatham, South London, the commuters appeared to give me a wide berth, possibly scared that I might say something personally to them. I let them push past me and escape down the platform. Following the crowd out of the station I began wondering what was holding things up. People were moving very slowly.

I was both shocked and disgusted when I realised what was

happening. There, outside the station entrance was a woman's body on the floor and people were actually stepping over it. I couldn't believe what I was seeing! Just beside the body was an elderly Scottish woman crying and appealing to the crowd for help.

"Tell me she's going to be alright son!" the elderly lady whimpered, absolute fear and desperation in her eyes. I grabbed her hand. Every bit of first aid training went right out of my memory. "Right....... um ... *recovery position*.... um ... *mouth to mouth*, how many times are you supposed to do that resuscitation thing?" my mind raced.

I looked into the woman's eyes; they were staring straight ahead. I had seen eyes like that before. My mother had been worried about a neighbour and asked me to check on her. I eventually found her in her bathroom. Pushing her body away from the bathroom door I made futile attempts to try to wake her up. Her eyes had the same look as this young woman. Sure enough the old lady was dead and now this young woman at my feet looked exactly the same.

"Tell me she's not dead" came the pitiful plea from the older woman. "We've only just left the doctors." I felt for a pulse. Nothing! Just as I was contemplating doing CPR the ambulance thankfully arrived. I managed to ask the paramedic if she was in fact dead. "Not yet mate but if we don't get off to hospital she soon will be!", grunted the ambulance guy. Apparently the older lady was her mother. The daughter had visited the doctor but had collapsed as she walked home. I agreed to meet the mother at Accident & Emergency in Croydon.

"She's dead son, she's dead!" the old lady sobbed as I got through the hospital door. "Come and see her!" She pushed me behind the curtains. There was her daughter laid out like a wax model. "You can give her a wee kiss if you want to son!" encouraged the mother. I kissed the daughter's forehead thinking, what a bizarre evening. I never expected to have shared such an intimate moment of grief with a stranger.

As I went to bed that night I felt numbness. Yet along with the grief there was also a strange sense of encouragement as well. *"Keep preaching Linds, people need to hear what you've got to say."* The gospel truly is a life or death message. At the wake, the Scottish mum introduced me to the family. "Here's the angel God sent along to help." I certainly didn't feel like an angel! I had felt very inadequate if anything, but I did believe that God had sent me along that day both to help that dear old lady and also to teach me a vital lesson. *"Even if they appear to reject your message, keep preaching it Linds, keeping preaching it."*

Keeping going, despite your fearful thoughts!

If we let our mind rule us, we will think of any excuse as to why not to talk to someone. "He looks too busy, she's in a rush! That one just doesn't look the type! That one looks too intellectual!

That one over there, with tattoos and muscles bulging all over the place, is definitely the type to bite my head off!" All this type of thinking will shoot into in our mind. It is often in our mind that the battle is won or lost! If the devil cannot attack our spirit he will certainly attack our mind with negative thoughts. Do the opposite! If the devil says 'don't talk to them' then go ahead and talk to them. The Holy Spirit may prompt me to cross the road to talk to a bunch of young people. I have learnt that, if I stop to question the initial thought then I will tend not to obey. In will come all those secondary thoughts persuading me to walk on by. I have 'blown it' thousands of times in this way. However, when I do obey the gentle prompting of the Holy Spirit, it is then the excitement starts.

Resting In the Spirit

Some people have advised me that I need to 'rest in the Spirit' and only to witness to people that God brings along. They point out that Jesus only did what he saw his Father doing. I seem to recall John Wimber telling the story of how he saw the word 'adultery' on the forehead of the man sitting next to him on an aeroplane. He was able to turn to the guy and quietly share this bit of personal information with him. Of course, it had quite an impact! Having your ear to God's Spirit in this manner can create a very efficient style of evangelism

    "Wait on the Lord! You are too manic in your approach!"

chided one Christian. "You need to wait on the Lord and let Him bring people to you!" I decided to give it a go. I have to confess, it did work but it was agony for me.

I had been standing in the entrance hall of our local further education college and was just about to share Jesus with a girl standing next to me. "*Wait on the Lord*" my mind told me. (My Christian friend had obviously got to me.) I waited for a few minutes and then thought how stupid it was. Jesus said '*go and preach*' and here was a girl next to me that I could talk to. Still, I thought I would give the Lord a few minutes to do something and even then I couldn't imagine what He was going to do. Was He going to get the girl, right out of the blue, to ask me a question about Jesus?

Suddenly the door of the college burst open and in came a group of students from a local Bible college, Bibles under their arms and carrying hundreds of Christian leaflets. "Here have one of these! This will tell you how to get saved!" It was like a whirlwind. All of us were 'machine gunned' with leaflets in 20 seconds flat. Then, as quickly as they had arrived, they disappeared again into the refectory, leaflets flying everywhere.

"Wow" said the girl next to me, "what was that?" Talk about Jesus handing things over to me on a plate! Off we went talking about the Lord, salvation and everything. Wonderful!

Over the years I have come to realise that we just have to put ourselves in a relaxed state of mind and let the Holy Spirit take over. My own rule of thumb is to witness to everyone unless they clearly don't want to know. I do ask God to bring people specifically across my bows. As I walk into a pub I ask God to point out to me anybody that he may especially wish me to talk to. If he doesn't attract me to one specific person then I talk to anyone who will listen. Sometimes the person who looks like they will be the least interested turns out to be the very person God wanted you to talk to.

It's very important to keep yourself in a state of prayer. Sometimes people may come with me when I am carrying the cross through their town. I love to have company but I sometimes get a little frustrated when they want to make conversation all the time. "Do I know this Christian or that Christian?" they may ask me. I don't want to be rude but often I can end up missing the first ten people because of having to listen to my Christian friend's conversation. We need get on with talking to the first person that comes along. If we get all picky or choosy we can sometimes end up never talking to anyone!

Keep going, even if you 'blow it'!

While carrying the cross near Aylesbury, Buckinghamshire I went by a whole bunch of men working by the side of the road. They were having their break and were happy to receive a cartoon Christian leaflet about Jesus. One of the men was sitting in his car eating his sandwiches, buried behind his newspaper. "He obviously doesn't want a leaflet!" I thought and decided not to bother him. Ten minutes later as I carried on along the road I saw a car parked in front of me with one of the workers that I had just passed sitting on the bonnet of his car scowling at me.

"I'm in trouble." I thought, dropping the cross from my shoulder.

"Why didn't you give me a leaflet?" the man bellowed. "You gave all me mates one and avoided me." I began to realise that the guy 'tearing a strip off me' was the man I'd seen in the car, reading the newspaper.

"I didn't think you were interested!" I said limply. "Not interested?" he repeated. "Well I am interested! Why on earth are you carrying that cross?"

I began to share my story. He then began to soften and confided in me about his own life. He hadn't been happy for a long time and had tried living in Canada. He then really opened up.

"I nearly went forward at a Christian meeting in Canada but there was a woman evangelist who was leading the meeting and I just couldn't ... well, I guess it's my pride ... I just couldn't....." (I think I knew what he was trying to say and so I helped him out.) "You couldn't let the woman lead you in prayer because of your male pride!" I stated. He began to nod his head. There was pain in his eyes.

"Well I'm a *bloke* mate, and not a woman!" I said with a

smirk on my face. "Why don't you and I pray together now and you can do what you should have done in Canada!" We ended up kneeling by the bumper of his car. It was a bleak stretch of road and the wind whistled past my ears while that dear man surrendered his life to Jesus. He stood up with tears in his eyes. Gone was the pain, replaced instead by a look of relief!

Next time you hear that voice, *"Don't talk to that one, he won't be interested!"* Do the opposite!

Even if it seems nothing happens, something happens!

Faced with the enormity of the need in some Asian countries it can often make me feel very under qualified and inadequate for the task. People with sometimes awful disfigurements line up for prayer and they really expect something from me. I often feel a fraud and wish another man with an anointing of healing was at my side to take a lead in these situations.

"My burden is light", says Jesus. We can pray for healing but it is God who does the supernatural. I often tell people this before praying for healing. This is partly so that God (not me) will get the glory when God touches them. It is also helpful to remove myself of any heavy sense of responsibility that somehow I must be at some sort of faith level before God heals. My job is to be right with God and to have just enough faith to believe for healing. It is *God* who heals! Remember that often people in poorer countries can have more faith for healing than ourselves. God is responding to their faith not just ours (which can be pitiful at times).

I recall praying for many sick folk in Bangladesh. There was a long queue. Initially, I was praying for bad backs and poorly stomachs (possibly the product of hard labour and dirty water). My faith level could just about cope with that! However, suddenly standing before me was a man with half a face. Perhaps he had fallen in a fire as a child? I gasped involuntarily as I saw him and my faith went out of the window. I believed (in theory) that God could give him a new face but I honestly had no faith to pray for that. The man was looking at me expectantly. I had to do something. In the end I just hugged him. "Oh Lord, touch him! Jesus, touch him!" I prayed as I held on tightly to this dear man. I felt that I had let him down but to my surprise the man was overjoyed and clung to me. At the end of the day *love* is the greatest gift to a person and that man felt loved that day.

I have prayed for many people who do not appear to have been healed. If only one out of ten people have been healed; that one person was worth it. If I hold back because of my lack of trust in God, then how can I be a drainpipe of God's power?

When I was a child I suffered with severe asthma and my parents would sit with me as I struggled for each breath. There were long nights of anxiety and desperation. Sometimes I would grasp onto my dad's strong hand as I heaved for breath. This somehow would give me strength to keep going.

My experience is that God doesn't always take away the suffering. In Sri Lanka we saw a stroke patient touched by God and in Bangladesh a few years later we were asked to pray for a husband and wife who had both suffered severe strokes. It was a pitiful sight, the man lying on the floor paralysed, his wife in a similar condition on the bed. His family had called us from the road to pray for them. With the Sri Lankan experience our faith level was high and yet, to our disappointment neither the husband nor wife appeared to have been healed on this occasion. However, at least the family knew that we loved them enough to pray our hearts out for them. This type of love can be like my father's hand giving the strength and comfort to keep going.

Despite the apparent 'failures' on the healing side I keep offering to pray for people. I decide to 'go for gold' in my prayer. Even if it is for a new face, new arms, new legs I have decided to pray for it. If Jesus did miracles 2,000 years ago I believe He can do them again. I am going to keep praying for the sick and if God does anything spectacular then I will be the first to say God did it and to Him be the glory.

Some who are not healed physically claim to have felt the Holy Spirit's presence when we have prayed. Some may experience nothing at all. Even if there is no apparent supernatural touch, at the very least people feel loved by the person who is praying for them. We are not called to understand everything but we are called to pray at all times! God is love and even if it appears that nothing happens when we pray, something *has* happened and people will have experienced something of God's love through you.

You will get opposition!

All of a sudden, Union Street was upside down and I was landing on my back on the tarmac. One minute I was giving a short preach at a bus stop to a bunch of Plymouth party goers, the next minute I was somersaulting, the cross cart wheeling next to me. This type of incident usually happens like lightening. There is often little time to protect yourself.

"Leave him alone!" screamed the girlfriend, "can't you see that the poor little chap is a nutter", she added, as she sought to pull her boyfriend away. The boyfriend was still cursing at me. "Where was God when my mate was being blown to pieces in the Falklands, answer me that?" shouted the guy. It was no good trying to reason with him, he was just seeing 'the red mist' and nothing I could say could calm him down. It was 1987, only five or so years after the Falklands conflict and together with a few pints of alcoholic drink to fan his feelings into flames; I was to be butt of his anger towards God.

I meet many like this; they are angry with a God they don't believe in for taking away a parent or a child. Life isn't fair at times and we all tend to feel that it should be! There is barely an ideal time for our loved ones to die. Hurt and grief quickly turn into anger and who gets it in the neck? The very God who suffered terribly Himself as He witnessed the death of His own Son. The very God who had the power to stop this suffering yet went through it for our sake!

Often I will try to understand where the angry guy is coming from. "Life has hurt you pretty bad hasn't it mate?" I might ask. Sometimes the very man who is intent on pouring his anger on me will totally change after I have prayed for him. I always try to talk to *the little boy* behind *the big man*. How many of us feel just the same as we were when we were a child? Now that little child has a big body and is supposed to cope with all that life throws at him. I understand that, during the First World War grown men could be heard crying for their mums as they lay dying on the battlefield. Men feel that society expects them to 'take it on the chin' but inside they can be hurting badly. When someone takes the trouble to pray for you, it often touches *the child* in you, the part in you that is crying out to be understood and to be comforted.

When someone prays for us, we can sometimes feel the *comfort* of the Holy Spirit and this causes the dam to burst. Lonely tramps invariably weep after I pray for them, especially if they are a little drunk. I have seen many men who have been greatly moved after prayer. Maybe their marriage has broken up;

maybe they have never had a father's love. Initial opposition can melt when they realise you are actually on their side.

However, there is also a *spiritual opposition* which is when people show a strong aversion to Jesus. Some try to explain this away rationally, "Oh, he probably has had a bad experience of church or thinks that you are trying to stuff religion down his throat." That may contribute to matters, but I have found that people are either for Jesus or against Him. Some people are violently against Him, they just don't see the need for Him what so ever! Others are very polite about it. At the end of the day, both are rejecting Him

The New Age followers, humanists or Buddhists often tell me that they have no problem with Jesus' teaching; it's just that *'they don't need an encounter with Jesus, to love people'*. I have met many good people who don't claim to have a relationship with Jesus. Sometimes, however, their very goodness can cause a blindness concerning their own sin. Without the plumb line of Jesus, there is no sense of falling short of a perfect standard. "I've nothing against religion, each to his own." It sounds so reasonable, yet it is a polite form of opposition.

Nearly thrown out of Glastonbury

Remarkably, the very farmer who established the festival at Glastonbury saw me carrying the cross on the site and wanted to have me removed. Almost every form of religious or spiritual practice is welcome, in fact, encouraged at the Festival and yet a man carrying a cross must be opposed.

I told the farmer that I had been praying for him and his family (they were going through a very hard time with serious illness at that time). This seemed to soften his stance towards me and he reluctantly let me stay. It is ironic, that when the filmmakers produced the Glastonbury film as a gift to the farmer, they included a clip of the 'cross man' walking by.

"I will not have the name of Jesus mentioned."

The Principal of the local F.E. College had my wife and I sitting in his office. I understand that he was a well liked Principal who was good to his staff; however, he was incensed that my wife and I had talked to his students about Jesus. "I will not have the name of Jesus mentioned on my campus", he growled, thumping his desk for effect. I felt like I was watching Hitler throwing a temper tantrum, I could hardly believe it.

I sensed the Lord urging me to tell the Principal that I loved him. "But, I feel anything but love for him, at this moment", I argued. I had been sharing Jesus at the college on and off for 20 years and now this enraged Principal was fixing to throw me off the campus for good. I asked God to give me love for him. There was no sentimental feeling of love; I merely decided to show him love.

"If I was an American, I would say, I love you man" I said,

shaking his hand as I left his office. "I am not American but I am still going to say I love you ... and you will still see us talking about Jesus to your students, just outside the gates of your college" ,I added with a twinkle in my eye.

You will get opposition, sometimes violent, sometimes polite; both come from the same source. Hardest of all, is when it comes from within your own home. How many couples have found that they have had a row just before they planned to go out sharing the gospel? How many parents have gone out to share Jesus and have perhaps seen great things happen on the street only to be confronted with a major crisis with their teenagers when they come home? The devil hates street evangelism and gets angry when you decide to do it!

Amazingly, sometimes the opposition can come from the church itself. I wonder how many ardent Christians have sought to get the gospel out on the streets only to be discouraged by older 'more mature' Christians? They might be told that 'they are not old enough', that 'they don't know enough', that 'they are not under authority', or that the 'church isn't ready yet to reach out'. Another subtle diversion, is when Christian leaders say that; 'we should pray about doing it before we go out'. Some churches find themselves praying about street evangelism for years before ever doing it. Usually, they never end up doing it at all!

Some pastors are convinced that street evangelism doesn't

actually work. "Our church is into 'friendship evangelism' or 'incarnational evangelism'!" There is no place for street evangelism. I've heard it all! Such attitudes and arguments can be so discouraging! They can act as an effective form of 'wet blanket', serving to quench the fire in our stomachs, if we let it. Usually the underlying problem is that the leader is uncomfortable about working on the streets himself and is therefore not convinced that people can respond to Jesus in this kind of 'cold contact' manner. Some pastors find our very enthusiasm, threatening.

We must not their opposition put us off. It hurts, to be discouraged in this way, but we mustn't let our hurt turn to bitterness! It might even make you feel like giving up on the church. Don't! Forgive and pray blessing on those in opposition and *go out and do it anyway*. Let the Holy Spirit encourage and comfort you! He will honour you for your faithfulness!

CHAPTER 8

ANGELS AND OTHER MESSENGERS

"Don't forget to be kind to strangers, for some who have done this have entertained angels without realising it!" (Hebrews Chapter 13 Verse 2 Living Bible)

"The Angel of the Lord encamps around those who fear Him, and He delivers them." (Psalm 34 Verse 7 NIV)

The Polish angel

I was too ill to do anything but curl up inside the van. I had suffered with glandular fever years before and every so often I would feel the same symptoms coming on. Today was one of those occasions!

We had been walking through Poland with the cross and had stopped by a small hill that was a memorial site for a Jewish wartime ghetto. The Nazis had slaughtered everyone in the ghetto and then demolished the area, burying the bodies under the hill of rubble that had been piled up. My friends on the 'Berlin to Moscow' walk had decided to pray at the top of the hill. I elected to rest quietly in the back of the support vehicle. However, as I tried to sleep, I was aware of people scurrying by the van, running up the hill to find out what was going on.

A short time later, my friends returned with an incredible story. When they had seen so many youngsters arrive, one of them, Bob Humphries, decided to preach to the crowds.

"Anybody speak English here?" he asked. "I do!" said a young boy with remarkably vivid blue eyes that seemed to sparkle.

The gospel was preached and duly translated by the special young boy and many responded. However, when my friends went to thank the boy, he was nowhere to be found. Was he an angel?

The street angel

In Romania I gave my lunch to a similar young boy in his early young teens. He too had amazing blue, bright sparkling eyes that shone with love towards me. He was so pleased to receive my food and prayer. As I left him I couldn't help questioning, was he also an angel?

The beautiful angels of Bangladesh

When I preached to the crowds in Bangladesh there would often be one or two extremely good looking people who would radiate with joy as I preached. They shone out in the crowd. They would usually get excited when I reached the point of describing Jesus' sacrifice on the cross for us. An old man gently put his arm around me in a Moslem village in Assam and as I looked into his face I saw those beautiful watery loving blue eyes again. Who are these people? Are they angels?

The old man of Kandy

In Sri Lanka, my friend, Dave, was carrying the cross into Kandy along with my friends, Thomas and Colleen. At the time, I was looking after Debbie who was hospitalised in Kandy's Seventh Day Adventist Hospital. My friends were finishing the walk with the cross for me.

We had been warned not to take the cross to the town of Kandy since it was viewed as the 'Mecca' of the Sri Lankan Buddhists. It was felt that this would greatly offend them. Sure enough, as they entered the outskirts of the town some guys on motorbikes began waving their fists and started shouting, "We are going to the police!" Deb then received a phone call from a very anxious Thomas, indicating that it might be necessary to contact the Embassy since it looked like trouble was brewing.

What happened then was quite remarkable. An old man appeared before them and went over to Colleen saying, "God is very pleased with what you are doing!" "You have children, don't you?" he went on. Thomas and Colleen were running an orphanage in Bangladesh at that time and had left their children in the care of a young girl from our church while they were in Sri Lanka. "You have no need to worry about them, they are fine!" The old man was so full of peace and continued to gently encourage them before disappearing into the crowd. Was he an angel?

The Kennington 'angel'

I was on the last tube train of the night. I had been preaching
on the platform to hundreds of Saturday night revellers. It was
my last preach of the night and I had just managed to deliver
it despite a whole load of heckling from several drunks. When
I got on the tube train to go home I remember feeling pretty
disheartened. Was it worth it? Was it worth constantly pouring
my heart out to a public who couldn't care less about Jesus? I
sat slumped on my bench in the train. Perhaps I should give
my 'tough guy' Jesus-leaflet to the man opposite. I decided I
wouldn't bother, thinking that he wouldn't want to know either.

I looked again at the man facing me. He was a black guy
and he was staring at me intently. Suddenly he leaned forward.
"You're thinking about giving up!" It wasn't a question, it was a
statement. I was startled.

"You're thinking of giving up!" he repeated. "Don't! Hang
tough, that's what it says on your leaflets. Jesus was tough,
you must be tough, now keep going and don't give up!" He
kept going on in this vain for a few minutes, and then abruptly
stopped. What authority! What insight! Who was this guy?

"You're ... you are ... you're right, absolutely right!" I said,
struggling for words. He wasn't moved or impressed by my
affirmation.

"I know I am right, now hang tough!" he concluded matter-of-factly, and then got off the train. "I've just seen an angel!" I thought, "An angel wearing glasses with black skin!"

I did keep going, convinced that God had sent an angel to encourage me. However, a year later I was catching the tube train at Kennington Station, and who should walk by? My angel!

"Oi, mate!" I shouted.

Hardly the right words to address an angel! However, it stopped him in his tracks.

"Oi, mate, you're that angel bloke who spoke to me a year ago ... you told me to keep going!"

"Yeah man, you're the guy who preaches on the tubes!" my angel replied, grasping my hand.

"I ain't no angel man" he chuckled, "I just had a message from God, that you had to keep going ... did you?" I nodded my head, feeling a little embarrassed for thinking for all this time that he had been an angel. However, in another way, it kind of didn't matter that much to find out that he was human. He was still a messenger sent from God, sent to encourage one of His servants. I always preach that God loves us but, to my shame, I am often surprised when I am on the receiving end of His love. Do I really believe He loves me?

God protects us over and over again. We are often unaware of how many times He protects us on a single day. On the roads, while I carry the cross His angels work overtime. In Russia I had just given a man a leaflet and turned around to see a car heading straight for me. I still don't know why it didn't hit me. In New Zealand a car appeared to actually swerve towards me intent on running me over. He missed. As I say, in Asia, there is probably more chance of being killed by crazy driving than by extremists.

The Hindu brothel

The team were exhausted and needed a day off. They had been working hard all week as we'd walked from Kathmandu, preaching and praying as we went. A hotel was found and the team sought to make themselves at home, washing their clothes and taking much-needed showers.

However, the night before, the driver of our support vehicle had received a dream in which he had seen strangers not only sleeping in our beds but also rifling through our belongings. He had felt that this was a warning from God and had happened to share it in the morning with one of our team. However, later that day he left us for the night, to visit his parents.

After enjoying a meal at our hotel, the team returned to their rooms to find that there belongings had been tampered with. It transpired, to our horror, that while we had been eating up stairs, our rooms had been used for the purposes of sex. I later learnt that as part of the Devali celebrations, it was custom for young men to have sex with prostitutes prior to 'worshipping' at the ornate temple across the road from the hotel.

'No nonsense Jenny' (the intercessor) sprang into action,

ordering everyone to reload the jeep. We weren't going to sleep in a brothel! God had warned us and we were off! The only trouble was, not only had our driver gone A.W.O.L. we also had no idea where we were going to sleep that night.

Resembling a scene out of 'Dad's Army' our female 'Captain Mainwaring' took charge. Ensconcing herself at the driving wheel she set off into the night with the jeep full to the gunnels with our ragged platoon and cross strapped on the roof rack.

"We've no diesel folks, it's been on empty for ages now!" announced Jenny. Fuel Stations are few and far apart in Nepal and we were in trouble.

"Pray!!" The order obeyed; all we could do is trust. However, just after we prayed Jenny saw the needle visibly rise from empty all the way to the quarter full position. Phone calls had been made and a local pastor directed us to a proper hotel in which to stay. The team could at last relax in safety, thanks to our loving Father!

The Angel of the Lord encamps around those who fear Him

I remember being reassured with this verse as I tried to get to sleep in a park in Nice in France. We were on our honeymoon. We had missed the last ferry to Corsica and had decided to sleep out in our double sleeping bag in the park near the ferry terminal. The only obstacle to our romantic night was that the park was not deserted at all.

My newly married wife Debbie was drifting off to sleep cuddled up to me when, to my horror, I spotted a crazy guy darting from tree to tree like a mad demoniac. He hadn't spotted us at that time but it was only a matter of time before he did. I prayed, I prayed hard! Debbie would freak out if I told her. As I prayed that beautiful verse about the Angel encamping Himself around those who fear Him slipped into my mind. A sense of peace and security enveloped me and before long I was fast asleep ... but not for long!

Suddenly I was awake, wide awake, adrenalin pumping and my hear thumping loudly in my chest. Staring down at me was the crazy guy only inches from my face. I reached out to shake his hand and as I did so, Debbie shot down to the bottom of the sleeping bag.

"Are you cold?" I asked in French.

"Oui" he replied.

"Are you on your own?" I went on.

"Oui" he replied, "et vous, et vous tout sol?" (Are you alone?)

At that point, my French gave out, because I found myself saying, "No I am not alone, I am with my husband who is in the sleeping bag." I had meant to say 'wife' but my French got muddled up. My mistake paid off. Understanding that there were two guys in the sleeping bag he looked really alarmed and ran off into the night.

Chittagong – Crazy Man

It is especially good to pray for protection after witnessing a particular move of the Spirit. There can sometimes be a backlash afterwards. The forces of evil aren't always that happy when their territory is invaded.

In Bangladesh, we had taken a group of 'Youth with Mission' students out on the streets as part of their Discipleship Training. We had just experienced an amazing act of the Holy Spirit in the town's central park.

I had just told the students that I wouldn't talk to anyone that day; it had to be *them* doing the talking. It was, after all, their training exercise in street evangelism. In Bangladesh people are often attracted to a Westerner. Not too many Westerners choose Bangladesh as a holiday destination so we were a bit of a novelty. Beggars who were perhaps hoping for good pickings were also attracted to us! I didn't therefore want to draw any attention to myself but wanted the students to engage with people themselves.

"I want to talk to you." Standing there in front of me was a crazy guy, his eyes rolling around in every direction.

"Where do these guys come from?" I thought. "Why do they always pick on me?"

"I want to talk to you", he insisted.

"Well, I'm not going to *talk* to you," I found myself saying, "I'm going to *pray for you* instead."

The next instant, I was praying in tongues for him. It was a powerful tongue and I can only presume that God was doing something quite significant in the man's spirit. No sooner had I finished praying when the wild man put his arms around me and gave me the most powerful bear hug ever. I feared that my ribs would be crushed. Just as I thought I wouldn't be able to breathe much longer, he dropped me and slipped down to kiss my feet.

"You can't kiss his feet!" someone shouted angrily. "He's not God!" I couldn't do too much about the man's act of worship because I was hemmed in by the crowd. However, I needn't have had to worry because the man had now pulled himself to his feet. He actually looked remarkably different, with calm, clear, peaceful eyes. Gone was the crazy look. With a new air of dignity he addressed the crowd.

"I have been searching for God for a long time. Today this man has introduced me to Him. He is my spiritual father and that is why I am kissing his feet."

It was Jesus who had touched Him and set Him free. As usual, I was just 'playing catch up', trying to make sense of what was going on. During such times I just feel like a fly on the wall, looking on, as the Holy Spirit *does His thing*!

Coming down to earth (literally), I immediately began looking round to find my wife. In all the chaos she had disappeared into the centre of a large crowd. Apparently she had been called over to pray for a young boy who was sick and was just lying limply on his mother's knee. After praying, she suggested that he be given an orange. On eating the orange, the boy seemed to revive amazingly quickly. The crowd were thrilled.

These New Testament-type happenings were so exciting. On the way home however, Deb found herself walking several yards behind me. Suddenly, a demonised man made to walk straight through her. It was terrifying. At the last minute however, an unseen force pushed the man violently to the side. Deb was so grateful to one of God's angels for protecting her. However, afterwards I 'got it in the neck' for walking on ahead and not protecting her myself. Whoops!

Working on the streets with Jesus does not necessarily mean that we will not suffer. Sometimes Paul the apostle was protected, other times he suffered. Whether the Lord helps us to go through times of suffering or whether He sends 'messengers' to protect or encourage us, He is still caring for us either way.

CHAPTER 9

JESUS GOES BEFORE US

Expected in Serbia

We had just got through the border post into Serbia when a plain clothes policeman arrived. He took one look at the cross and within minutes we were being told to leave. A few days later we re-entered Serbia, hiding the cross in the back of a van. Only a few years previously, 'Christian Serbs' and 'Muslim Bosnians' had committed awful acts of atrocities against each other. I guess it was felt that carrying the cross may be particularly provocative and serve only to fan into flames antagonism.

I was lost without the cross and was complaining about this to a friend as we walked in the suburbs of Belgrade. Nevertheless, we prayed for opportunities to share Jesus even with those who couldn't speak a word of English.

At the corner of a street stood a 'Rasputin-look-alike' sporting a long beard that flowed all the way down to his chest. On seeing us, he grabbed us warmly and with a heavy Serbian accent, greeted us in English.

"Come with me my friends, come and meet my wife!"

He lived at the top of an old block of flats. As we climbed the stairs to his flat we explained how we were praying for Serbia and that it was our real desire to see people come to know Jesus. As my eyes adjusted to the darkness of his one-room flat I became aware that there was a figure asleep in the double bed which held central position in the room. As we entered, the figure sat up, it was his wife.

An excited interchange occurred between 'Rasputin' and his wife. I couldn't wait to find out what all the fuss was about. When I did find out, I was overawed.

Apparently, his wife had just dreamt that two Westerners would come to her flat and would talk to her about Jesus. That is exactly what we did! We didn't need to do too much talking either! Their hearts were ready and prepared for Jesus.

We have always to remember that, *as we* start walking, *Jesus* starts walking. Not only does he walk beside us, He covers our back and continues to work with those we meet. He also goes on ahead, preparing the way for us as we go,

People ask me about my strategy and technique. "We walk, we pray and *stuff happens.*" It really is, as simple as that. I often tell people, "It pays to be thick! That way, you don't have to worry too much!"

I am not saying that I do not believe in organisation. These walks are expeditions and require a high standard of preparation. Forget just one item of your kit and things can go pear-shaped. For example, I forgot my torch in Bangladesh and found myself having to walk 'by faith' in the pitch black of the night. I stumbled and nearly broke my ankle. A broken ankle in the middle of the night, in mosquito-ridden Bangladesh is no joke. Even with the best of planning, things can go wrong. People can forget to pick you up at an airport; all sorts of frustrations can assail you. It pays to be as organised as possible but then to put everything into God's hands.

Jesus sent His disciples with few human resources instructing them to accept hospitality and provision. They came back overjoyed. He had gone ahead of them and shown His power. God had *'done His stuff!'*

A Romanian restaurant owner was thrilled to see us arrive with the cross and he welcomed us immediately to a table in his establishment. We had experienced overpowering heat that day and we all smelt strongly of dirt and sweat. We were more than a little embarrassed to be guests at such a classy restaurant.

However, as we ate, the owner's son arrived. He could speak excellent English and we instantly liked him. He had deep questions, a profound thinker! It was plain that God's Spirit had been working on him and by the time we were slurping up our last few mouthfuls of soup he was bowing his head to receive Jesus. His face was shining as we left.

I usually order a New Testament in the language of the country in which I propose to walk. I then highlight the relevant verses so that I can use them to explain the gospel. I am always reluctant to give away this Bible as it is often my only way of communicating Jesus to the people who don't speak English. However, this young man so obviously wanted Jesus; I just knew that I had to give him my Romanian Bible. God had his hand on that young boy and had clearly prepared him for our meeting. Jesus had gone before us.

Brussels encounter

In Brussels I was relaxing in the evening with a friend after having carried the cross all day. I was in 'switch-off' mode. We should always operate on 'stand-by' mode, never on 'switch-off"! However, that evening I wasn't reckoning on trying to talk to anyone, I was totally exhausted. Even so, I have a habit of greeting everyone I meet and as a young man walked past me, I naturally said, "Alright, mate?" The guy stopped dead in his tracks. Colour drained from his face.

"How do you know I'm English?" he said in a strong North Wales accent.

"You're not English!" I said "You're Welsh, in fact you are from North Wales, probably from Anglesey!" (I originate from North Wales and recognised his accent.)

"How do you know that?" he blurted, his mouth dropping open. He looked furtively from side to side, his face etched with fear.

I quickly explained that I also came from Wales, mentioning the name of the small town in which I'd spent my earliest years. Immediately he let out a torrent of language which was neither Welsh nor repeatable. He was from the same town and had been best friends with one of my relatives.

"I thought you were the xxxx police" he said. It transpired that he was wanted by the North Wales police and thought that we were undercover cops. He expected to be arrested any minute. It wasn't so much the police but God who was seeking to *arrest him.*

Inviting us back to his flat, he began to explain that his life was in a mess; depression and suicidal thoughts were close companions. The devil was trying to destroy this young man's life. I felt great love for him. I knew his family and had played with his older brother as a child. It wasn't a mistake that I was now sitting opposite to him.

I implored him to let us pray with him. Even at the very suggestion, he started to shake and grab for his whisky bottle, pouring out a large glassful. There was no way that he was going to let me pray and he began to visibly panic. Usually I back off at this stage but I knew that I must pray for him. As I prayed he gulped down the whole glass in one shot; there was an incredible battle going on.

It would be great to say that he accepted Jesus. He didn't, but I do understand that he did eventually return home to our native Wales. I believe that our meeting wasn't just a coincidence but that God had gone before us. He had His hand on this young man and had arranged for us to reach out to him. Sharing the Good news on the streets, is not something that we do on our own, we do it in tandem with Jesus Himself!

The wink of Jesus

It was 1996, my first marriage was breaking up and I had said things I shouldn't have said. My wife had taken herself upstairs for a bath. I hated myself for being so full of anger. Inching myself to the edge of the settee I cried out to God, 'If ever I needed you, I need you now!'

Instantly, in my mind, I heard the click of the front door opening. I had started a very vivid daydream. In the dream I saw Jesus standing before me. He had dancing, liquid eyes that radiated joy and humour. How could He be so happy while I was such a despicable character, so selfish, so ugly and so hurtful? In His left hand He held a video cassette (this was before the age of DVDs). I thought that the video contained every single sin that I had ever committed. My eyes were riveted on Jesus as He went over and inserted the tape into the video player. I braced myself to see the awful truth of my sin displayed on the TV. The TV sprang into life and white freckles appeared on the black background as the tape began to roll. I waited, holding my breath, almost too embarrassed to look. The freckles continued. A minute went by, then another minute, then another… more freckles, just white flecks. It took several minutes before the revelation hit me. White freckles, just white freckles – the tape had been wiped clean, there was nothing on it. The whole message of the gospel hit me like a ton of bricks; the tape had been wiped clean. Every bit of nastiness, every bit of self-centred manipulation, every horrible detestable word of criticism, every lustful thought, everything, the whole jolly lot gone!

What an incredible relief!

I looked up to Jesus who was still standing in front of me, grinning like a Cheshire cat, pure joy oozing from His eyes. I suddenly felt totally, totally accepted by Him. I had initially wanted to hide from Him, feeling such shame. Now I just felt so loved, so accepted. Then it happened, Jesus winked at me.

'Sit down Jesus,' I blurted. Here was a friend who knew everything about me, yet I was loved enough by this beautiful man who radiated such joy, almost mischievous joy.

Just as I was settling down to have a good honest chat with Him, my wife came down from her bath and the daydream came to an abrupt end.

What had just happened? Was it a vision or a dream? I still don't know. All I know was that I received a personal revelation of the gospel. I am forgiven! I saw the laughing, joyous face of one whom I believe to be Jesus. He didn't wink at my sin in any way, but he winked at me in love, humour and joy.

I had another day-dream-type vision years later on the streets of Dhaka, in Bangladesh, at the start of my walk with the cross. I had started to feel a fear come over me while waiting to begin the walk. How would the crowd react? Would I be mobbed or stoned? My mouth was dry and something akin to 'pre-exam nerves' gripped me causing my stomach to feel as if it had knotted itself into a tight ball.

Just as I picked up my cross and slammed it down on my shoulder I looked to my right. There, standing next to me I found myself seeing in my mind the figure of Jesus. Ten feet tall, bathed in a yellow effervescent light and shouldering His own massive cross as well. There was that joyous face again and guess what? Yes, He winked at me again. "Are you ready?" I seemed to sense Him saying. I had thought that I was carrying the cross on my own but I wasn't. I was simply walking with my 10 foot Jesus. He was before me, with me and after me.

Some psychologists may say that this type of daydreaming is mind over matter. I just feel that if Jesus can communicate through dreams and visions to humans in bible times then maybe He can give vivid daydreams to simple guys like me. Even if these experiences are mind over matter, they still communicate effectively the wonderful gospel truth that Jesus loves us, has brought forgiveness, Jesus accepts us and has promised to walk with us as we pick up His cross to follow Him.

"Anyone who wants to be my disciple must follow me because my servants must be where I am. And the Father will honour anyone who serves me" (John Chapter 12 verse 26)

Where He is

Jesus is already on the streets and He can call us to be *where He is*.

"I am in a club, *come and join me.*"

"I'm sitting in the dirt with these old alcoholics, *come and join me.*"

"I'm in this bar with this lonely homosexual, *come and join me.*"

Jesus doesn't have barriers as we do.

"I'm in North Korea, Saudi Arabia, Bosnia, Chechnya, *come and join me.*"

For most of us, it is often our fear, our sense of life preservation, our indifference, or maybe our lack of love for Jesus that stops us from joining Him. We are not all called to work in this particular way but when we are called, we must follow!

"If any of you wants to be my follower, you must turn from your selfish ways, take up your cross daily, and follow me. If you try to hang onto your life, you will lose it. But if you give up your life for my, sake you will save it." (Luke chapter 9 v.23 and 24)

"I really envy you." a woman told me once. She was slim, elegant, her wrists dripping with jewellery. She had just shown me her Rolex watch, worth thousands. Outside was her sports car. She wanted for nothing. "I really envy you! You are so rich!" "I am rich!" I agreed. "What I have experienced of Jesus in this life has made me the richest man in the world!"

If we take our first faltering steps in following Jesus out into the streets, He will show us that He has gone before us. He is already there; He just needs your mouth to speak through and your eyes to shine through. He wants to embrace the world with your arms. He wants to make you rich, at His expense. Rich in love, as He flows through you, rich in joy as you see Him touch people, rich in peace as you realise that it is not you working for Him *but Him working through you.* May Jesus enrich you, *as you too join Him on the streets!*